* October 1973: One of two photomontages from Bristol City Docks Group first Report, on by far the most important area to become at risk during the period. The Group urged the City Council to adopt greater building densities, mixed uses, pedestrian priority, assessment of buildings and industrial objects to be preserved and architectural competitions as prerequisites and goals of redevelopment. Some ideas were taken up, but none actually materialised, least of all the distinguished urban form visualised here. Instead the character and actual fabric has been deliberately taken apart and now only awaits theming.

REECE WINSTONE 1909–1991　　*Summer 1988*

BRISTOL AS IT WAS 1963-1975

REECE WINSTONE
ARCHIVE PHOTOGRAPHS

Compiled by
John Winstone

Reece Winstone Archive & Publishing
Ilex House, Front Street
Churchill, Bristol BS19 5LZ

For X-MM, so young

Also by Reece Winstone FRPS

*Those titles marked with an asterisk are out of print. The remainder
are available direct from the publishers, some in limited numbers.*

Abbreviations

BAC   *Bristol Archaeological Committee*
B & G   *Bristol & Gloucestershire Archaeological Society*
BIAS   *Bristol Industrial Archaeological Society*
C16, C17 etc.   *Sixteenth and seventeenth century etc.*
CBA   *Council for British Archaeology*
CPAB   *Council for the Preservation of Ancient Bristol*
RFAC   *Royal Fine Arts Commission*
RW   *Reece Winstone*
SPAB   *Society for the Protection of Ancient Buildings*
VAG   *Vernacular Architecture Group*

*Cross references are shown in bold type by volume number
followed by plate number viz [**2/135**]*

ISBN 0 900814 70 5
© Reece Winstone Archive & Publishing 1990
Printed by Burleigh Press, Bristol

Second Impression with minor corrections, 1992

Compiler's Foreword

Reece Winstone presented his books of the post-war periods (vols 5, 8, 14, 18 and 31) first as a record and only second as an indictment of *civitas,* but the latter takes on an inescapable primacy after 1962. Others have subtitled the period under review the growth of public protest.[1] In Bristol, as elsewhere, high rise development offered attractions of open space around buildings and vehicles were granted free movement and the fullest penetration. Digestion of *Traffic in Towns* by Colin Buchanan published in 1963, with its consequences for preserving historic town plans and buildings, was unpalatable to Bristol. The Civic Amenities Act of 1967 provided for the designation of conservation areas, but Bristol was slow in making provision – the first area, Henbury, was not designated until January 1970. In fact local authorities took up lucrative Department of Transport grants for road building which they could couple with housing clearances and redevelopment without due attention to the Skeffington report of 1968 which provided for public participation in the planning process; and Bristol was no exception. The government-led high-rise system building that was proffered as the cure-all to slum clearance and the vested interests it spawned ensured many years passed before public disenchantment with this 'burnt out land'[2] became widespread.

It fell to few indeed to possess an appreciation of historical perspective of townscape and to fewer still the ability to expound it (the dearth of adequate terminology remains indicative of this) or to design with regard for what is now termed 'context'. Reece was one whose eyes were open to the official and private decision-making that was so disfiguring his much-loved city. Only by the end of the period could one find expert agreement on what constituted good townscape. The compiler remembers the late John Totterdill saying he had found it necessary to explain to his audience the difference between preservation and conservation. The Montague report on reuse of old buildings was still six years from publication at the close of the period. As an instance: if there had been majority agreement amongst architectural students of the opportunities for reuse afforded by Vanbrugh's derelict Kings Weston brewhouse in 1969 (it was a conveniently nearby training ground for the writing of delapidation reports), this was not the view of the lecturer who was unable to envisage a new use. And patently neither was it a view shared by the University authorities (the compiler led the opposition to prevent their demolition of Vanbrugh's 'Echo' loggia on the same estate) who held the lease from the equally disinterested Corporation-owners.

The decisions that were to have such an effect on Bristol's urban grain were often of long standing. The clearance of St Augustine-the-Less, of the west side of Georgian Lodge Street and in consequence the decline of the east side creating the threat of office development, and precinct zoning such as blighted Tankards Close and part of Kingsdown east of Horfield Road under crown immunity, are all cases in point. They all stemmed from decisions by officers facing reconstruction even before the war had ended. In the immediate post-war period only public resistance stopped the wholesale clearance of a large area of the city approximately equal to the whole of the area under the remit of the urban development corporation of 1989 – some 900 acres. Decisions of the moment were made with full knowledge of their implications (the preservation lobby saw to that), and were made blind to those representations and were just as ill-judged as those made twenty years before under more trying conditions. The disfigurement that ensued was extensive and became all-pervading, with little or no interest being shown in retaining what was known to be of value. The issue of conservation in Bristol during this period is discussed further in the succeeding section.

Reece's love of Bristol has lasted a lifetime. He has written that he felt his love of photography and experience in freelance journalism combined with and fulfilled his earlier career into a vocation as unofficial recorder. His first freelance article accepted for publication charted the progress of road improvements near his family home in Southville and this style of illustrated article on British buildings, people and customs was eagerly taken up by the editors of the popular pre- and post-war magazines. Reece admired John Latimer's achievements in *Annals of Bristol* most of all. It was Latimer's recording which spurred into life Reece's annual sheets entitled *Changes in the Face of Bristol* 1961–87 (not to be confused with his book of the same title, vol. 36) which he offered to readers. These have been expanded here, with a minimum of omission, to form the Chronology of Events. Conscious of the shortcomings and errors that such a chronology must contain the compiler apologises in advance for misrepresentations therein, or elsewhere, and welcomes corrections and suggestions for inclusion in a future edition.

It has been said of Reece that it was he who taught us to use our eyes to what was happening to Bristol[3] and that is probably true. This he did through his camera, lectures, letters to the paper, in committee of local amenity societies and the 'As It Was' volumes. He was impatient with local bureaucracy, which moved all too infrequently, no matter how extensive the lobbying. Success came infrequently and then was often only partial; *plus ça change.*

The 'As It Was' series is nevertheless a positive documentary and should not be viewed simply as nostalgia. This volume is no exception. All speak of the destruction of certain tangible and intangible qualities in urban fabric that go to make up a living city and whose study is now termed urban design.

Inevitably in Bristol we see first an 18th-, then a 19th-century expansion overlaying and juxtaposed with the medieval and post-medieval bases but the retrogression and maltreatment we are concerned with here is largely of the 20th century. This can be most easily seen in a loss of building density, greater space between buildings, greater penetration for vehicles and loss of mixed usage by the imposition of zoning. In the process much that is well-made, like stone surfaces[4] and the physical enclosure of site, is destroyed. Many of these qualities were characteristic concerns of the 18th and 19th centuries. They may have made for a different and presently unfashionable attitude to the ownership of property (railings and boundary walls are a case in point) but by providing visual enclosure they made for good townscape. Even today the majority of professional decision-makers cannot apparently differentiate between deterioration and the value of the principle enshrined – to them it is something worn, a defective encumbrance that should go. So it was then.

This book attempts to bring out these qualities whose loss, with the benefit of hindsight, appears all the more regrettable and unnecessary. It illustrates that process, the efforts made to stem the erosion and some of those organisations responsible. The skill lies in recognising, as the photographer did – for all Reece's own shots of the period were taken with the intention of publication – what was to be forfeit before the event, and in differentiating between what was an acceptable loss and what should be retained. Sometimes the loss is incidental, perceived as for a greater good, occasionally the motives are socially-minded; at other times it's sheer greed or official vandalism.

Reece's own photographic coverage tails off soon after 1970, when he was sixty and devoting all his available energies to publishing. Through the sixties at least twice a week, in early morning or early evening light (he placed great store by sunlight) Reece was out and about somewhere in the city with his 2¼″ square or 3¼″ × 2¼″ range-finder cameras getting one or two black and white negatives per subject. In the volume period he took some three thousand photographs of Bristol and only about one and a half thousand shots extending his previous livelihood, freelance coverage of the rest of 'Beautiful Britain'.

Forced retirement due to ill-health has prevented him from undertaking this 'last' volume,[5] beyond the initial selection of shots for each year in question made several years ago. Such is the significance of Reece's coverage of Bristol – thirty-three principal volumes covering the years 1840–1962, and indeed he was the first to publish photographs of such vanished scenes anywhere in 1957 – that it was felt that so ambitious a project should not be left uncompleted.

The compiler has been left to decide how best to formulate the book, the captions and the inclusion of any supplementary material such as has accompanied previous volumes. Although Reece proposed coverage of the period 1960–1975 it was felt better to leave his earlier volume 1960–1962[6] to speak for the early years and to concentrate on the subsequent years, knowing that these were already crowded and that Reece's volume-dating developed from successful publishing rather than a logical scheme. The partnership that has been formed to run and extend the Archive with an active collecting policy hopes future publications will be tailored to a combined date and geographic base and this too suggested a simple run-on of dates from the 1960–1962 volume.

Conscious of Reece's idiosyncratic choice of supplementaries in previous volumes the compiler has endeavoured to include something of Reece's own contemporary thoughts in the form of selected letters to the local papers to preface each year. No apology is necessary to include something by that *émigré* from another beleaguered commercial centre, Manchester, the architect John Totterdill, who made Bristol his home until an untimely death robbed Bristol of a real force, just as his influence began to be felt. His article on Temple Meads Old Station is included as much as an example of his approach as for its continuing relevance.

Reece has always realised the necessity to supplement his own coverage, even whilst he has been at his most active, so the Archive includes the work of other recorders. In 1974 the compiler purchased his first 35mm camera, an Olympus OM1, and his picture-taking starts in quantity from this date, shortly after his return to Bristol. This work is now also part of the Archive and it is fitting that some shots be included here. But as with previous volumes essential material missing from the Archive has been obtained expressly to fill-in omissions. Inevitably it is hardest to know when to halt printing-up negatives and how severely to edit. For the first time project work has been included for the influence it had, or should have had, on development. The photographs generally are presented in date order. However, certain events may be best comprehended through photographs taken in a preceding year. In such cases the earlier photographs are grouped with the principal coverage.

Demands of professional practice have curtailed the inclusion of a period map with locations of photographs superimposed. The intention is to provide multiple superimpositions through successive volumes. It is to be hoped that the map for this volume may be published separately and news of this will be given in a subsequent Newsletter. The continuing expansion of the Archive also provides readers with a greater choice of prints for purchase. For this reason the Archive welcomes the opportunity of acquiring old photographs for safe-keeping and dissemination by making prints available to readers. Those seeking copies should enquire of the publishers.

To all those who have gifted photographs to the Archive for this volume and in the past the partners are especially grateful, for without them the Archive cannot grow. Photographs by the compiler are asterisked before the plate number and those given to the Archive or the copyright of others are marked with †.

Our thanks to the following donors, lenders and those granting permission for us to reproduce their photographs: the late J B Appleby, D Balmer, Bristol Regional Buildings Record, Bristol United Press Ltd, Ms H Burrough, City of Bristol, M S Curtis, the late R E Edwards, J Hunt, A W Hunt, Ms D Jones, P Lewis, D Loader, Ms J M Maggs, T Organ, Port of Bristol, B Rome, Royal Commission on Historical Monuments (England), E H Skeele, Studio Para., D Vintner. And grateful thanks to the following architects whose drawings or work is included: R Bowden, D P Daw, J Johnson-Marshall, A Jones, A M Rome and J White.

We are grateful for the continuing help and expertise of Reece's printers, Burleigh Press. For photographic assistance we thank Cotters Photography; for Reece's letters to the paper and extracts from contemporary articles, Bristol United Press Ltd; for critical comment and information, D Dawson and D Lloyd; and for advice on the text, and tireless discussion, proofreading and the usual prerequisite of patience, my partner, Rosie.

John Winstone
Ilex House, Churchill
August 1990

Footnotes
1 Priest & Cobb, *The Fight for Bristol*, 1980.
2 Gillian Tindale's 1990 phrase on Radio 3.
3 Mike Jenner in conversation, 1989.
4 These are currently being put on computer in order that they may be taken up and 'rationalised' or put to 'more effective use elsewhere', contrary to long-established conservation practice.
5 Forty volumes in all were projected, of which two were not specifically about Bristol.
6 Available direct from the publishers.

Corrections to Second Impression
Pl. 15   Little Peter Street
Pl. 24   Waiting Room off right pl.23
Pl. 103/104   Cater Stoffell & Fortt
Pl. 374   VRT model ceased 1981, works closed 1983

The Burgeoning of Conservation in Bristol

In order that readers may have some perspective of conservation in Bristol over the review period, with all its shortcomings, and of how the situation has developed in subsequent years, the compiler offers this synopsis. It is very much a personal view, formed over many years' interest and involvement in conservation on behalf of three of the national amenity societies at various times and as architect and Bristolian, and there will no doubt be those who consider it contentious. It attempts, through the opinions of the compiler, to show a reverse for the shining coin of the public face of conservation in Bristol.

For a city of Bristol's size and pre-eminence it is remarkable that only some dozen buildings (a row in Colston Street, No. 30 St Michael's Hill, Blaise Castle, those mentioned in the next paragraph and the Manor House at St Michael's Hill) come readily to mind as having been conserved to date in the true sense of the word. It is all the more remarkable that this should be so through the conservation-conscious 1980's.[1]

Of this count of historic buildings why do only five buildings come to mind as having been repaired within the period 1963–75 – St Nicholas, St Peter's, Temple church, Baker's Hall roof and the interior of Abbey Chambers? From 1963 there were very few architects practising conservation in Bristol and for some of these such work was a part-time activity as provincial practitioners. Building preservation, as it was commonly referred to at this time, was a rarefied subject, considered a rather eccentric and obscure 'specialism'. In many aspects the contribution to be made by conservation was not only not understood, people genuinely did not know what might be involved in the process or have any comprehension of the end result. Nor would the public have known it or known how to judge it had they seen it, whereas there was wide agreement of the wrongs of wholesale clearances of Georgian areas. These were the days when mortgages for old houses were simply unobtainable. Only a handful made the blind, grant-less leap into run-down Georgian houses; few would have attempted a move into a C17 house in a city. And there were of course few publications and no DIY industry to guide, or perhaps misguide.

The great C19 recording of standing medieval and post-medieval structures in Bristol started by Braikenridge, extended by E W Godwin, Venn Gough, T S Pope, Alfred Hudd and John E Pritchard, had petered out with Denning. In 1938 CPAB commissioned Ralph Edwards, a doyen of Bristol architects practising well into the period and one of seemingly only two local architects pre-war with the historical perspective and capability, to compile (and later extend) a list of historic buildings worthy of preservation. But if the cause was to be effectively served post-war in this most commercial of cities another approach was necessary. H St J O'Neill's safeguarding of various Bristol buildings by scheduling them as ancient monuments was one such approach. National developments post-war in assessment of early buildings were few, if trail-blazing. They included Fox & Raglan's interpretation of the sequence of styles and techniques of early buildings in Monmouthshire (published 1951) and the formation of VAG which became active in 1954.

Conservation as a subject has always been ill-defined, with uncertain boundaries and forward-reaching goals and this is not helped by inadequate terminology. Proper conservation in the compiler's view consists of a particular approach or 'working with the building' together with the essential implementation by like-minded craftsmen. The plan-form and circulation around the building which inform the architecture and give meaning to it have to be respected, as do the existing openings and structural systems of support. It is necessary to adequately assess fabric and condition prior to formulating appropriate schemes of repair and reuse. Such schemes require retention of historic interiors, retention and repair of historic fabric without recourse to replacement in replica and any necessary additions to be kept subservient in size and scale, designed in a contemporary idiom and not in pastiche. Partial demolition should not be entertained as the corollary to defective structure and strenuous efforts have to be made in order to avoid ensuing degradation. Facadism is not conservation, nor is facelifting. Retaining the existing fabric of the historic building is the best way to maintain its character; needless replacement and replication degrade listed buildings because their historic importance is in some part removed in the alteration. Most of these points and further guidelines are set out in Department of Environment Circular 8/87 Appendix IV.

In the 1960's preservation was a more frequently used term, often loosely employed to encompass conservation as well and preservationists grew pejorative overtones. The ill-advised 'restoration', which should have been more clearly understood post-Morris, continues to be used (and practised) indiscriminately. Nowadays of course everyone professes adherence to conservation and the word is a catch-all. Yet there would still seem to be no real *understanding* amongst the public of the complex issues involved. As a result a host of untoward circumstances grew out of the review period; we had the Civic Society advocating the moving of historic buildings to obviate loss, regardless that Bristol buildings are wholly or partly of rubblestone. Then, surprising as it may seem, none of Bristol's precious timber-framed buildings had their frames repaired to the tenets of the SPAB (still the case today). And the widespread belief sprang up that the practice of replica construction and pastiche design were acceptable substitutes for retaining surviving historic fabric and for contemporary design. This, and the undue importance attached to the facade of a building, probably springing from the need to secure the hundreds of decaying historic buildings, resulted in consents being granted to facade considerable numbers of buildings. Little was written by the few designers who were equally at home with historic and new work, and the two in conjunction, to dispel these serious misconceptions.[2]

Bristol was not considered an historic town in the first survey of English towns and so the translation of private list to statutory list was low priority. The then minister for Housing and Local Government, Anthony Greenwood MP, wrote of the new provisions for conservation areas in January 1967: 'If we are to preserve anything of the old scale and the old architecture, we can only do it as part of urban planning. So it was fitting that my predecessors, the ministers responsible for planning, should have been given the task of drawing up "the List", that list of buildings of special architectural and historical interest on which all our preservation efforts have rested. Being "listed", I fear, means only that a building is not inadvertently destroyed; it does not ensure that any use can be found for it. We are planning now for a much more active system of preservation, for a combination of legal, administrative and financial measures that will enable us to keep all that is worth keeping, and to dovetail new building into it in a way which looks good and is good to use. Local authorities now play a leading part in this work and they will have to continue to do so. Their record is highly uneven . . .'

In the interregnum of the statutory list for Bristol, signed in 1977, the old Grade III buildings had no protection and notification of their demolition was not even a requirement (a constant bug-bear to amenity societies for the Corporation declined to notify prior to demolition), the newly-funded College of Advanced Technology, Department of Architecture (becoming the University of Bath school in 1972) set up a regional buildings record with an architect-director and one researcher in December 1962. In 1964 the City of Bristol Museum's curator in technology commenced recording the industrial archaeology of Bristol and region on behalf of the CBA and College of Science & Technology.

The educationalists too were surprisingly slow in recognising conservation as a subject, with neither Bristol nor Bath School of Architecture (the latter then in Bristol, at Kings Weston House) including the subject in their diploma and degree courses. The now defunct Bristol School of Architecture eventually started an extra mural conservation course in 1980. This gulf still persists generally in architectural education today, and only now are moves being made to introduce the best conservation practice in curricula. Conservation-inclined architects locally were left to teach themselves what constituted conservation as best they could. The take-up of interest that found fresh adherents in the 1970's did not generally extend to established practitioners and a distinction was soon perceptible between those entering practice in the 1970's and the previous generation.

It was not just the schools that failed to encompass building conservation. The local amenity societies failed to make any substantial headway too, in so far as their committees made up in the main of voluntary serving non-experts may give direction to building owners frequently disinterested in conservation or influence the professional, particularly on the question of the 'how' of conservation, on the critical test of what is best for the building. Too often grant was the only means of wringing something out of an otherwise unsatisfactory proposal. When historic building grants became substantial and this could be coupled with VAT advantage for alterations developers had a whole new shopping bag to open. The loser was invariably the historic building.

The arrival of the national amenity societies in Bristol from the late 1970's with their local groups or local caseworkers was not greeted with much enthusiasm. There was then an opportunity to construct a dialogue with the five national amenity societies, applicants and the planning authority which did not materialise. Generally the representations resulting from referrals to the five national amenity societies were not insisted upon in granting consents and this is the picture throughout broadly more than half of the planning authorities in England today. The Conservation Advisory Panel, formed in 1977, which might have been a means for achieving conservation on a project by project basis, was too frequently disregarded at this detail level. Influence in respect of schemes for historic buildings locally has tended to be exercised by policy control, rather than by advisory publication, teaching or example in the City's substantial estate. Repair schedules, used to control the most sensitive issues where a proposal may be inadequate, often appear to miss those matters of detail which go to inform the whole building.

In the period under review there were plenty of professionals who rallied to the press, even to the extent of publishing their own local magazines, on issues of comprehensive redevelopment, traffic segregation and municipal provision, but this group was by and large absent when it came to the future and treatment of historic buildings.[3] The conservationists had yet to overcome the hurdle of obtaining alternative schemes which they could use in opposition. It was some time before these began to be gifted by their own professional members. The City Museum archaeology department carried out destructive recording through digs as opposed to interpreting and preserving standing medieval fragments intact. The planning department began to grant conditional consents in return for archaeological work, but this meant little for conservation if the standing structure was then demolished. Even the Museum Advisory Committee lost its independent voice from the influence of the Council House.[4]

The casualty of Ashton Court was a great pointer in the Corporation's estate soon after purchase in 1959. The SPAB report of 1960 that recommended various uses be found for internal wings was not heeded and the Court was reduced in order to lessen chronic difficulties with rainwater disposal, demolishing some of the oldest parts and C19 additions of distinction. The 1971 architectural competition in the main compounded, rather than repaired, these losses.[5]

To all intents and purposes conservation in the first half of the review period was not practised in Bristol, and Bath was effectively little better off, although occasional advice was sought from within that city. By 1970 proper conservation was still a rarity in Bristol but by then the calling-out for change did not fall entirely on deaf ears.

Corporate owners found ready sites for new construction or, in the main, were content to lease what developers were building. Trustees with almshouses and the like faced, or rather mostly didn't face, the need for conservative renovation. St Nicholas' Almshouses, except for the loss of its high stacks, had been a notable exception as early as 1961.[6]

The accelerated declaration of conservation areas through the latter part of the period and on through the late 1970's and 1980's was greeted with hope and growing interest as a mitigating influence on development, but the Corporation had been slow to first seize upon the provision that the Minister had made to so designate. By the end of the period the coverage city-wide was approximately half in area what it is today, some 11 areas compared with 29 to date.[7] Toward the end of the period however it appears to the compiler that some designations were being made not just in order to conserve the historic areas but to hold influence over the appearance of new buildings, a constant bug-bear of the Civic Society.

The clearances above King Square for high-rise council housing had met with cries of derision and the processes involved are documented elsewhere.[8] The critical years for Kingsdown had been 1956–8, but the City architect's high-rise design was not published until 1963 and the City press officer's revealing comment at that time, 'The picturesque is seldom comfortable and rarely convenient', was almost as good as John Betjeman's plea in 1957: 'This airy suburb, this place of Georgian view-commanding terraces, trees, cobbled streets, garden walls and residential quiet, is all the more attractive for its unexpectedness so near the middle of Bristol. I hope that Bristol Corporation which has in its trust the most varied, and to me, the most beautiful large city in England, will spare Kingsdown. Such a unique district can never be replaced.'

Tragic too for the period was the neglect afforded the Georgian suburb centred on Portland Square. St James's Square was an unnecessary casualty of the City Engineer's planning of Broadmead, and there had been previous, pre-war attempts to be rid of the square. The remaining intact Georgian conservation area based around Portland Square was given the impetus of outstanding status but such early enthusiasm was not backed up with grant provision until the much later Joint Conservation Programme. The prerequisite of recording interiors was not undertaken. Buildings were simply left to rot, open to the mercy of vandals. The developers who moved into Brunswick Square, the first part of the area to be rehabilitated, were given consent to facade one terrace (despite the public inquiry decision requiring that the whole terrace be retained) and when this was found to be acceptable to the planning committee other developers started to do likewise in Cumberland Street and others nearby.[9]

The movement toward direct action in Bristol, so characteristic and scene-changing of the early 1970's, took many forms and alliances from the Campaign against the Outer Circuit Road to occupations of office buildings in defiance of homelessness by the Joint Housing Action Group and its corollary, a two-year moratorium on office consents. The Town Meeting of 15th December 1969 halted, if not immediately, the Corporation's proposed suspension of navigation and the reclamation of parts of the Floating Harbour and gave birth to the City Docks Group[10] and City Docks Ventures Ltd.[11] In the city docks the denuding of a conservation area has been at its most visible with buildings demolished since designation in 1975 without architectural assessment or over-much concern for whether they were listed or listable, and new housing built without any regard for the results of the architectural competition submissions, [12] such that the area has become a cypher with 'Historic Harbour' signs on motorways. It only remains to be themed!

By 1975 the need for building conservation had entered public consciousness; it was something 'funny architects' did,[13] even if it was far from being the widely accepted byword of the late 1980's. By 1975 some of the original specialists had retired, but the list of practitioners was extended through the addition of young, self-taught adherents. The younger practitioners, short of conservation commissions, rued established practitioners obtaining large conservation commissions which they believed were outside their elders' ken and would not be delivered. One of the unfortunate consequences of the city being the regional centre for design was that unsympathetic treatment was directed on to vernacular buildings in the hinterland and countless hundreds of buildings suffered.

The exponents of serious conservation in Bristol wrote virtually nothing on the subject locally (excepting perhaps statements hidden from public consumption in those most *recherché* of repositories, proofs written to defend historic buildings at public inquiry against professional protractors) and this remains so to date. There was certainly no local publication to carry the gospel.[14]

The statutory list when it came in 1977 had been many years in gestation, so long (seven years) that it was said that it must have been a part-time job! The shortcomings of the new list were two-fold. It came too late and omitted many buildings of some quality but considered marginal, many of which have since been demolished. Among its suggestions for inclusion the City apparently submitted for consideration historic buildings threatened with demolition for road-widening![15] Under reorganisation in 1974 the responsibility for listing passed to the County of Avon, whose officers were proficient. Bristol appeared to take the view that the contents of the list were a matter for the DoE (or their agents) and there appeared to be an ambivalence towards it. This has devolved down to the present position where the planning department often fails to instigate requests to spot-list buildings, seemingly puts too low a priority on interiors and internal alterations when considering listed building applications, preferring to address conservation in its more prominent public face – facadism, replication and facelifting.[16] At public inquiries concerning listed buildings the need to give the necessary weight to proper conservation can appear to be lacking. [17] It is unfortunate that enforcement action to ensure the stock of listed buildings is not compromised appears to be given lower priority than matters involving breaches of planning control.

The arrival of public protest never effectively settled on the treatment of historic buildings in Bristol and the targeting of alterations has been so comprehensive and the damage so extensive that physical unpicking of the mistakes is frequently no longer worthwhile or practical. Such historic building cases, with the difficulties they bring, were often beyond the abilities of local amenity societies. The national conservation societies, which statute requires be consulted, were in the main not heeded when they intervened.[18] Consequently their representation dropped off as it became clear to them that the planning department did not intend acting on their views. Their local groups were yet to come (Vic Soc 1978, SPAB 1982, Georgian Group 1986) but by and large this has changed things very little, with one or two exceptional cases where the national society has declined to be worn down, although even these cases have proved the obstacles set against them rather than conserved buildings.

Footnotes

1 Literally hundreds of listed Bristol buildings have been degraded since 1975 owing to unsatisfactory conservation, often with the benefit of grant aid. Examination of the buildings so treated are outside the period covered by this volume.

2 Shoreland House, a block of modern flats in Beaufort Road, best illustrates the ineptitude pertaining on new work in conservation areas 1975/6. The planning department stipulated that a well-known and inappropriate rough faced concrete block of artificial stone be used for this new work in Clifton. It required the intervention of an RFAC commissioner to arbitrate on a more suitable material in order to overcome the stalemate that was holding-up construction.

3 Ashton Court was an exception in *Bristol Forum* No. 3.

4 Local government contracts of employment obligate staff to their employer's view.

5 The compiler, with three others, submitted a solution aimed at preserving the whole complex intact.

6 The debacle over the City Cultural Committee twice refusing to meet CPAB over Lewin's Mead Chapel beggars belief – CPAB minutes Feb. 1971.

7 I am grateful to T Organ for reminding me that Bristol has so far escaped the 'big money' that today is producing vastly over-sized schemes in other cities. Clearly conservation area status will have an increasing part to play in this regard. Yet it has not prevented the Crown playing an invidious game with listed buildings (demolished contrary to provisions of government circular 8/87 Appendix IV) for new law courts in Small Street.

8 *The Fight for Bristol,* Cobb & Priest 1980.

9 The facading and replica building process of listed buildings in Cumberland Street, Portland Square, St Paul's Street and Pritchard Street is now 75% complete and was a scandal of significant proportion (see, for instance, CAP minutes 21 July 1989).

10 City Docks Group sought housing in preference to offices in the docks, conscious of the landscape value of such a site, but sadly their assessment was diligently misinterpreted and a stage-set of most unprobable and damaging ilk has been in process of construction now for a number of years.

11 Formed to prevent the sale of cranes on Princes Wharf for scrap.

12 Post-war architectural competitions have had a sorry history in Bristol revolving around a lack of public display of all entrants' schemes (viz. Ashton Court, Baltic Wharf Housing and WCA warehouse). For a history of C19 competitions, see Appendix III in *Bristol: an architectural history,* Gomme *et al.*

13 Personal communication by a commercial estate agent.

14 *Avon Conservation News* publication attempted quarterly to fill the gap that the wider audience sorely needed, but this was not born until 1977.

15 Personal communication. Road schemes are one of the few instances which listing is usually powerless to stop.

16 See a debate on the differences between officer views in Bristol & Bath in *Avon Conservation News* No. 23.

17 On occasions the conservation case is not made at all at inquiry e.g. 6 & 7 King Square, 1990.

18 Interestingly a recent volume *(Design Control in Bristol 1940–1990,* Dr J Punter 1990) devoted to the design of post-war office development in Bristol sought to record the views of the conservation lobby, but signally failed to interview the practitioners of real conservation, the casework-members of the national amenity societies or their national secretaries.

CHRONOLOGY of EVENTS

1962

November
Bristol Regional Buildings Record formed to collect photos and drgs of buildings of architectural merit

1963

January
St Andrew-the-Less, Hotwells, being dem.
Cumberland Basin site: all houses dem.
Quakers' Friars: old mortuary dem.

February
Bishops Palace ruins: Dean & Chapter decline to build to east or incorporate standing walls in new school hall. C14 work dem.
Pollard's Hat Shop, Old Market St, closed
Christ Church City church hall, Pithay, dem.
Hotwells Road/Merchants Rd east corner dem.
Castle St: Co-op site cleared
Latimer's tombstone repaired by public subscription

March
Nos 21–23 Clare St: new offices opened
Clifton Hill House extension completed
Beeching Report on railways published

April
Cumberland Basin cranes erected over New Cut
Ashton Park: trees cut down for approach road
Clarence Rd: Mayor's Arms dem.
Morley roundabout reduced in size
Quakers Friars: Planning & Public Wks Comm. set up Permanent Planning Exhibition
Kingsdown: City Council intent on dem. against Georgian Group, RFAC & CPAB representations
Berkeley nuclear power station opened

May
Eastfield Rd, Westbury-on-Trym: bottleneck removed [2/51]

Morgan's Corner becomes Colmer's Corner
High St shut for widening; re-opens 18th Nov.
Nos 4 & 5 Broad Plain saved from dem.
Rownham fountain removed
Giles Schacht, the Clifton Chemist, closed down
Clarence Rd: Mayor's Baths dem.

June
Muller Rd/Gloucester Rd traffic lights installed
Upper Maudlin St: dem. of north side commenced
Queen's Rd/Triangle West: controlled crossings installed
Rownham fountain trees cut down
Whiteladies Rd supermarket opened
Hotwells Rd/Merchants Rd west corner dem.
Little Theatre: last performance by Rapier Players

July
Redland Hill House School closed
Tyndall's Park: new 30 ft lampstandards erected
Victoria St/Redcliff St corner set back
Coronation Rd/Clift House Rd south corner dem.
St James' Barton: controlled crossings installed
Ashley Rd/Picton St corner: dem. of Georgian house

August
Regent Cinema dem.
Nos 37 Welsh Back & 11–12 Queen Sq. dem.
Sheene Rd, Bedminster: bottleneck removed near site of tram depot

September
Queen Sq.: rebuilding of former post office
Redcliff Hill: last house dem. on sw side
High St/Wine St corner: traffic lights removed for new roadway
Park Row: remains of Coliseum wall dem.
Empire Theatre & Tatler Cinema fittings sold

October
Temple St/Philip St corner: gabled houses dem.
Southmead Rd/Wellington Hill West corner: Waterdale House dem.
St George fountain: traffic lights installed

Newfoundland St/Pritchard St west corner dem.

Mary-le-Port St carriageway taken up [4/52]

Frogmore St: Entertainment Centre, planned 1941, starts on site

November

Embassy Cinema closed

Feeder Rd widened under railway bridge

Queen's Rd: site above nurseries cleared

Bedminster Bridge convenience dem. [1/57]

Regal Cinema, Staple Hill, converted to Bingo hall

Nos 38, 40 & 42 Granby Hill dem., following dem. of No. 44

W-o-T horse trough removed

St George: rebuilt library opened

Queen Sq. closed following gale damage to trees

No. 13 Thomas St (scene of a murder) dem.

Stoke Hill: Eastmead Court, 15 flats, completed

RWA School of Arct. becomes a Univ. Dept, fated to be victim of University cuts in 1984

Brunel House (formerly Gt Western Hotel): threat of dem.

December

Bank of England opened

2nd Bedminster Bridge opened

Approaches to new St Philip's Bridge cleared

Bristol Airport: during '63 runway extended to 5,250 ft

Bush Training Centre for mentally subnormal opened during '63

1964

January

Prof. Buckminster Fuller lectures to BSA & arct. students

Prince St: Nos 28, 30, 32, 34 & 54 dem.

Stokes Croft: No. 106 dem.

Embassy Cinema dem.

Bedminster Down Rd: widening up the hill

Henbury Rd/Falcondale Rd traffic lights installed

St Nicholas St: Queen Victoria fountain basin missing

Quay St: Walsh's building dem.

All Saints St: Fry's 1902 building dem.

Station Rd, Henbury: school dem.

Prewett St: Proctor's interesting window removed

Whitchurch Lane: Rowe Bros open new offices & warehouse

Redcliff Way: scheme to realign on Portwall Lane with overpass at end of Redcliff St & commercial block on podiums of church

February

Park St: Folk House, independent adult educ. centre, opened

Pithay: HMSO (formerly Fry's by Sir G Oatley) dem.

Corn St: Royal Exchange building dem.

Quay St: remains of St Lawrence Church open to view

Brentry: dual carriageway opened

March

St Thomas St: Nos 30, 32, 34, Georgian houses dem.

Bath St: 'Georges' lettering to Counterslip taken down

Dowry Pde: Lebeck house dem.

Pembroke Rd: part of ruins of All Saints' Church dem.

Redcliff St: Buchanan's Wharf cleared

Tower Hill west side cleared. Council declines to reprieve Shot Tower, earliest extant brickwork in city

Brislington: The Shrubbery, C17, under threat

Easton: comprehensive redev. on Radburn segregation principles

April

Brentry: Knole Lane widened. Charlton Rd flats under construction

Bedminster Down Rd/Winterstoke Rd corner set back

Stoke Lane, W-o-T: site cleared for new shops

Castle St: Nos 53A–58 (Hinds to Greig) dem.

St Anne's: 120 ft high elec. pylons erected

Pen Park House severely fire-damaged

Bellevue Rd: St George Health Centre opened

May

Maudlin St: Univ. Dental School opens

Parson St/Bedminster Down Rd: permanent one way system

Deanery Rd: Folk House dem.

Bristol Hippodrome tower dem.

Cathedral: Latimer memorial receives inkwell & quill

June

Lower Lamb St: request to incorporate buttresses of Abbey Barn in library extension failed in previous year. Med. buttresses dem.

July

Cumberland Basin: Harbour Master's house dem. and first Swedish 80 ft lamp-post erected in Britain

Gloucester Row, Clifton Down: BTCC gates removed

Brislington: C17 house Seven Gables dem.

F C Jones dies

August

Broad St: Nos 29, 30 & 31 dem.

Christmas Steps: Victorian lampstandards erected

Queen's Rd: Gordon Bay Hotel dem.

Castle St: last shop (Burtons) vacated, dem. May '65

Henbury: Norton Farm dem.

St Nicholas' Church nave shell re-roofed

September

2nd parking meter zone operative

Berkeley Sq.: se side cleared

Rownham House dem.

Colston St: no left turn at top

Duke St dem. [3/178]

Durdham Park made into cul-de-sac

College Sq.: green railed off to run with Cathedral School

TSR2 cancelled (maiden flight April)

October

St James' Pde: Nat. Farmers' Union Mutual Ins. office complete

Temple Way/Victoria St: Bristol Wagon Works (latterly Henley's) dem. [8/27]

York Rd: Methodist Church ruins, near St Luke's, dem.

Downend: Clevedale, C17/C18 mansion dem.

Hobbs Lane, Denmark St, dem.

Bridge St: last two houses dem.

Rock Court, Berkeley Pl.: City Engineer declines to retain

Labour party wins general election; H Wilson PM

November

Christmas Steps/St: corner house repaired

Park Row: Prince's Theatre ruins dem.

Empire Theatre dem.

Harley Place, Clifton: 19 flats completed after RFAC amendments

Housing Act 1964: £350 grant for 5 standard amenities; £500 discretionary grant for conversion to flat

December

Henleaze Rd: Nos 177–205 (Georgian cottages) dem.

Cumberland Basin: new roadway under flyovers opened

Queen's Rd: carriageway divided to make extended one-way system round the Triangle

Bath St: Beard's bookshop closing down sale

Survey of Industrial Archaeology of Bristol Region by Museum's Centre for Study of History of Technology, on behalf of CBA/Coll. of Science & Tech. N Cossons leaves Bristol end '68

Office Dev.: Floor Space Index applied to control large developments

St George Health clinic opened during '64

1965

January

Upper Maudlin St: Thornhill Place hoarding removed, dem. May

Kingsdown: Thomas St closed for new road system

Carey's Lane: Tatler Cinema dem.

L B Johnson US President; Sir W Churchill dies

February

St Stephen's Church clock removed

Henbury Rd: Lodge to Henbury Hill House dem.

Arno's Castle Bath House remains dem.

17th & last issue of *Bristol Weekend*

March

Cathedral restoration commences

Temple Way opened from Victoria St to St Philip's Bridge

BRI Hospital chimney erected on site of old maternity hospital, a Georgian house in Southwell St

Westbury Rd: Southey House blank (tax?) windows unblocked

Clifton Down Rd/King's Rd: terrace dem. for new shops

Mill Lane, Bedminster: Gents' cast-iron convenience, of Glasgow make & 1 of 4, threatened. Re-erection declined on cost grounds.

April

Cumberland Basin bridges & flyovers opened
Bristol Airport: terminal and runway extended 750 ft

May

St Peter's churchyard cleared
St Philip's Bridge: single line traffic
Kingsdown: Spring St & sw of Dove St dem.
Victoria St/Temple Way: new slip road opened
Bloomfield Rd: new British Oxygen boiler house
Bristol Civic Society: 60 years old. Plan to close Deanery Rd
Bedminster Down Toll House: City Engineer declines to reprieve
CPAB deputation to City Council calls for City to prepare their own list of historic buildings for preservation! (All Grade III buildings could still be dem. without prior notification)

June

Counterslip transferred from Countess Quay to Victoria St new road
Station Rd, Henbury: Aviary dem.
Colston St: pawnbroker's at top of steps to The Artichoke dem.
Kingsdown: Lower redev. started, 347 dwellings, £1.3m John Laing (Construction) Ltd. 'The picturesque is seldom comfortable & rarely convenient' (City press officer)

July

King Sq.: Institute for Deaf completed
Frogmore St: Leopard Inn dem.
Colston St: Chapel of Three Kings restored
Ashley Down Rd: Tudor Lodge roofless, dem. March '66
The Hippodrome entrance canopy dem.
Broad Quay: Cruickshank's (Willway's) garage dem.
Pile St: railway bridge dem.
Lodge Street: several houses dem. sw side
Easton: large areas dem.

August

Little Theatre (formerly Lesser Colston Hall) receives raked auditorium in lieu of rear balcony

September

Penpole Point: Portway Secondary School opened
Queen's Rd: Students' Union opened

October

University Walk: proposals for School of Mathematics publ.
St James' Sq.: fire at Roydon House
Victoria St: Lowman's Black Boy tobacco sign removed
St James' Barton/North St: corner property collapses
St Mary Redcliffe: restoration completed
Temple Meads Old Station listed following CPAB request Nov. '63. Listing of Brunel's bridge over tidal Avon requested

November

Hanbury Rd: MoHLG Good Design Award for 14 elderly persons' units
High St/Bristol Bridge: traffic lights installed
Broadmead: Dorothy Perkins shop redesigned
Bus numbers change
Julian Rd: church dem.

December

Dean Lane, Bedminster: Spring & Chatham Georgian cottages dem. for RC school development
Yellow bins of road grit set up on steep slopes
Rock Court, Upper Berkeley Place, dem.
70mph speed limit imposed on British roads

1966

January

Park Row: viewing seats removed
Feeder Rd: lock-keeper's cottage dem.
Brislington Hill: Gothick lodge dem.
Wapping Rd: level crossing rails taken up
Queen Sq.: Nos 14–16 (corner Mill Ave) dem.
Filton: new roundabout & new road opened
METHOD building exhibition at Building Centre

February

Cornwallis Cres.: La Retraite School wall collapses

Gloucester Rd/Berkeley Rd: garage dem.

Victoria St: Yeo Bros & Paull (previously lowered) dem.

Temple Meads Old Station: car park in Brunel's train-shed

March

The Park, Frenchay: Civic Trust award for terrace housing

Central Library extension foundation stone laid

April

Shirehampton Rd: 6 spec. shops & flats

Haberfield St: tannery dem.

Brightbow Bridge: controlled pedestrian crossing set up

Arno's Castle: Barnard's Museum displays Lowman's Black Boy

Development Plan for city publ.: includes inner & outer circuit roads

May

Christchurch Primary Sch., Clifton: 1st METHOD sch. in city

Castle Park: pre-contract drgs started for museum & art gallery

Pennywell Rd: contract placed for 169 houses & maisonettes

Collison Rd, Hartcliffe: contract placed for 12 shops/maison.

Withywood Secondary Sch.: contract placed for extensions

Pipe Lane: Nos 2, 3 & 4 dem.

St Thomas St/Mitchell Lane: warehouse dem.

Coronation Rd: Nos 29–34 dem.

Broadmead: Fairfax Hse fire, paternosters taken out of service

York Rd: houses from St Luke's Rd to Bath Bridge dem.

Warwick Rd: many houses dem.

Portwall Lane: south side dem.

St George's Rd: Prince Albert Inn dem.

June

Kingsdown: 347 high rise flats & maisonettes 'proceeding apace'

Bower Ashton: W. of Eng. College of Art under construction

Barton Hill: tenders rec'd for 111 high rise council dwellings

Gloucester Rd/Berkeley Rd: chapel tower dem.

July

Victoria St/Cart Lane: Veales dem.

Hotwells: Simon Short's fountain renovated & resited opposite Clifton Vale

Whiteladies Gate: shops on west side dem.

Horfield Barracks dem.

Saftey, 'last' Severn Trow refloated, but grounded for final destruction. Owners, Thos. Silvey, make model. '67 rescue bid to save bow fails

Henbury Swimming Pool opened

August

Portway: dual carriageway works commence

Orchard St: re-roofing & restoration of Georgian houses

Royal Hotel: portico dem.

Colston St: embankment under repair

Old Market/Temple Way underpass 'nearly completed'

September

Severn bridge opened

M4/M5 interchange at Almondsbury opened

Cumberland St/Upper York St corner dem.

St Michael's Hill/Perry Rd: traffic lights installed

North St, Stokes Croft: west side dem.

Eastville bus garage (former horse-tram depot) to close

October

Fishponds: Methodist church 1894 dem. for a supermarket

Pithay re-opened

Tower Hill Ambulance Station completed

Park St freed of congestion

November

Feeder Rd: Avon Bridge re-opened

St Philip's Bridge re-opened

Old Market St/Lawford St corner widened

Mill Lane: Capper Pass Smelting Works dem.

Old Market St: White Hart (Empire entrance) dem.

Whitehouse Lane, Bedminster: 1st industrial unit erected in redevelopment area

Frogmore St: Entertainment Centre 806-seat cinema opens

Tower Lane (Broad St to Small St) re-opened

Lawrence Hill: Kerswell's shop (inventor
m/cycle combination) dem.

December

Upper Berkeley Place: gale blows masonry off
six buildings, crushing seven cars; site
cleared

Castle St: closed, 25 ft map on hoarding taken
down

Queen St widened

Old Market St: underground conveniences
dem.

Deanery Rd/St Georges Rd corner (formerly
Ship Inn) dem.

St George Tram Depot: Manchester collector
takes away 1895 lines

Ellbroad St: last house dem.

Avonmouth: new sewage treatment works
opened

1967

January

Henbury Hill Quarry closed

Upper Maudlin St dem. for hospital

Commission on Bristol Historic Churches
invites contributions

Orchard St: brick facades painted over.
(Pennant kerbs painted '89)

February

Old Market: old houses adjoining Omnibus
offices dem.

Portway: central reservation laid down

Stoke Park Rd: new University Halls (Badock
& Lower Wills)

Deanery Rd; raised pavement prevents traffic
using Norman arch

Brislington Hill/West Town Lane corner
widened

March

White Tree painted red during Rag Week

Oxford St, Kingsdown, dem.

Queen St/Castle St re-opened after widening

Avonmouth Rd: houses dem. for M5

Portway: new car park for tennis courts

Queen Charlotte St: building site St Nicholas'
Schools

Narrow Plain & Sloper Lane dem. for
Temple Way

B&G & CPAB's joint Bristol Archaeological
Committee becomes Museum Advisory

Committee on Bristol History after 11 yrs,
with RW as Secretary

April

New Police HQ & Courts opened at
Bridewell

St James' Sq.: two houses with shell porches
empty

Westbury College: interior restored

Frogmore St: multi-storey car park opened

No. 21 Portland Sq. (E W Godwin's
birthplace) redeveloped

Fishponds Vicarage dem.

May

Lodge St: Countess of Huntingdon's Chapel
dem.

Barton St: Derham's old Boot Factory dem.

Victoria St: work commences on prefabricated
flyover

Long Ashton Bypass: Yanleigh Lane viaduct
piers cast

Ashton Gate: flyover completed

Henbury Bypass: works begin opp. Blaise
Hamlet

Windsor Terrace: stables below retaining
wall dem.

Lower West St, Bedminster: National School
dem.

Old Market/Carey's Lane: excavation for
underpass starts

Horse Tram body found by RW at Downend
used as fruit store

June

King St: No. 47 dem. [4/59]

No. 40 Baldwin St: Mansfield's building gone

Hallen: great activity in motorway
construction

Park Picture House, St George, dem.

St Michael's Hill: Nos 126–132 dem.

Parking 'meter maids' (19) on the streets

July

Broad Quay: Bristol & West building opens

Temple Gate: buildings opp. station
approach dem.

Central Library extensions opened

First sonic boom tests

No. 12 Lower Park Row: dem. follows roof
collapse

August

Tucker St dem.

Westbury College: after partial fire Georgian
house dem. by National Trust!

Henbury & Hallen joined by new road
St James' Sq.: No. 10 dem.
North St, Stokes Croft: three cafes closed
Christmas Steps: two antique shops rebuilt

September

St James' Church: west front restored
Victoria St: prefabricated flyover opened
St James' roundabout: almshouses & former
    Register Office dem.
Cumberland St: St James' Hall dem.
Avonmouth Docks: Call Stand ended;
    decasualisation introduced
Smoke Control Programme: 7th of 21 areas
    declared for completion in 1980

October

Church Lane, St Michael's: houses dem.
No. 89 Park St: Budd plaque unveiled on
    George's bookshop
Terrell St & Horfield Rd, east side, dem.
Victoria St: buildings between Temple St &
    flyover dem.
Police Stations to be closed: Horfield &
    Fishponds
Central area: 24 hrs no parking, except at
    meter bays
The Hatchet Inn, Frogmore St, being
    extended

November

Portway, below Sea Walls: civil eng. work
    removed
Hampton Rd: No. 98 (home of W Venn
    Gough arct.) dem.
Yellow boxes at traffic junctions laid out
No. 52 Cumberland Rd & almshouses nearby
    derelict
Clifton Down: gas lamps fade away
Ashton Swing Bridge dem. commences
St Andrew's Park bandstand dem.
Colston Ave: Sun Assurance (Oatley &
    Lawrence) under threat
Ashton Turnpike empty: St Mary Redcliffe
    Vestry asked about its future
CPAB request conservation area designations
M32, Parkway: planned in 3 stages, the
    Newfoundland Rd/Ashley Rd stages both
    to be elevated

December

Broadmead Baptist Church redeveloped as
    shops & church
Henbury Rd: one-way traffic past the Blaise
    Inn

West Town Lane/Bath Rd: traffic lights
    erected
BIAS formed: 1st Journal publ. '68

1968

January

Muller Rd & Stapleton Rd: houses at
    crossroads dem.
Cat & Wheel, Bear & Rugged Staff
    de-licensed
Old Market/Temple Way footbridge opened
St James' Barton roundabout: excavation
    commences
Pembroke Rd: Nos 13, 15 & 17 (Budgetts
    offices) dem.
Mardyke Ferry service ends
City docks: Port of Bristol boasts 41 quay,
    roof or derrick cranes, hydraulic or electric
    powered, with 360,000 sq.ft of warehouse
    floor space in 15 transit and appropriated
    sheds, and berthage for 17–19 vessels,
    6 berths being appropriated

February

Odeon Tower dem.
Police panda cars result in police station
    closures
Redcliff Hill: properties below The Ship Inn
    dem.

March

Park Row: University Drama Dept succeeds
    Vandyke Printers
Portway: new tall street lighting
PS *Bristol Queen* sold for scrap. Cultural
    Committee decline to purchase as docks
    museum

April

Alfred Hill: Granville House/Place dem.
St James' Sq.: east side dem.

May

Barton Hill: Gt Western Cotton Mill dem.
Clifton Heights: change of use to offices
Redcliff Hill: shops above Redcliffe Pde
    corner dem.
Muller Rd & Stapleton Rd: viaduct dem.
Avonmouth: Imperial Smelting Co.'s zinc &
    lead smelter opens

June

Cumberland Rd: No. 52 (Georgian house) dem.

College of Art: demonstrations repeat Hornsey College call for student involvement in course development

July

Metropole Cinema given over to Bingo

Old Market St: half of roundabout opened

Floods enter 3,000 houses in valleys of Malago & Trym; Northern Stormwater Intercepter extension planned into East Bristol for 1969; Ashton Stormwater Relief 1970; Malago Interceptor 1972–76; Bedminster Bypass Culvert 1971+

Avon St: John Hare's paint factory dem.

Coronation Rd/West End: house dem. for petrol filling station

Greyfriars: C17 house under threat of dem. Threatened with becoming a public footpath in 1989!

August

Bath St: old brewery with large lettering (Counterslip) dem.

Park Row: site of Prince's Theatre cleared

Easton Rd: Old Malt House dem.

Redcliff Backs: Western Counties Agricultural Co-op mill dem.

Mill Lane Sq. closed

Cock & Bottle Lane: archaeological dig on castle site

September

SS *Great Britain* return appeal opened

October

Temple Church: timber-framed rectory, windows boarded up

Redcliff Hill: Shot Tower interior dem.

Old Market St/Temple Way: underpass opened

The Centre: Guinness clock advertisement taken down

Theatre Royal: Georgian stage machinery under threat despite Bristol Theatre Royal Trust

November

Kingswood: Ten-pin bowling closed

Bristol Pottery to leave city after 316 years

Redcliff St: Mardons (formerly Wills offices) dem.

Mill Lane: cast-iron public convenience dem.; Museum takes parts

Severnside: Imperial Smelting Corp. (NSC) Ltd to develop 283-acre Trad. Est. ICI site includes fertiliser, anti-freeze, detergents, synthetic fibres, pharmaceuticals & chemicals

December

Roman Rd: cottages dem.

Police pocket radios supersede whistles & police telephone pillars

St Philip's: wholesale fruit market opens

Redcliff Hill: Shot Tower dem.

Brislington Hill: wall dem. for supermarket

St John's Bridge: police garage dem.

Long Ashton Bypass opened

Castle Park mound: work starts

Buckingham Place: garden renovation

1969

January

Temple Church Rectory under threat

City Council buys Nos 11–13 Guinea St for refurb. as houses

Bath Bridge: old building overlooking bridge dem.

Pen Park House: site redeveloped for housing

Portway–Avonmouth Rd: new roundabout

February

Redcliff Hill: carriageway on site of Shot Tower opens and Pets' Paradise dem.

Wells Rd crossroads widened at Broad Walk

Merchants Rd: Heber Denty timber yards disappear

March

Christmas St: Lindrea building dem.

Redcliff Hill: excavation for subway

Regent St, Clifton: Nos 40 & 42 under threat

St John's Steep: houses boarded up

Knoll Park, Almondsbury: tower under threat

Kingsweston House chimney arcade restored

Royal Fort music room restored

April

British-built *Concorde* maiden flight follows French flight

His Majesty's Cinema, Stapleton: renamed Concorde

Jacob's Wells Baths: modernisation
completed

May
Upper Berkeley Place: Dual carriageway
appears
Hotwells: Merchant's dock filled-in (1st wet
dock)
St Mary-on-the-Quay: application to
demolish (later refused)
Muller Rd/Parkway: traffic diversion
Small St post office opens philatelic bureau

June
Narrow Lewin's Mead: Willway's 1740 house
dem.
MoHLG (later DoE) prepares revised list of
buildings of special arch. or historic interest
(publ. '77). Only Shakespeare PH is listed
in 1969 in Docks area

July
W D & H O Wills presented with the
Hartcliffe Project Brief, to decant to
Hartcliffe by autumn 1973
Falcondale Rd: houses erected on line of
ring road
Brentry: 1st Pelican crossing in Bristol
Westbury-on-Trym: cottage adjacent library
dem.
Montpelier: St Andrew's Church dem.
Docks: proposed extinction of navigation
rights thro' the Float & New Cut, filling part
of Float & the Feeder for development

August
Lewin's Mead: Georgian house dem.
Greyfriars: C17 house dem. stopped
One-man operation buses commence
St Nicholas St: Queen Victoria fountain
privately painted up

September
Pembroke Rd: houses on site of RC cathedral
dem.
Queen's Rd shops start 6-day week
Bristol Polytechnic designated. 1st stage
tender accepted '72

October
Park St area: 3rd meter zone designated
Little Peter St: two public houses dem.
Newfoundland St: 1st NO RIGHT TURN
sign (to Pritchard St)

Union St: Broadmead Baptist Church open
spire hoisted
Baker, Baker Ltd (Retail) becomes McIlroy
CPAB requests separate posts for City
Engineer & City Planning Officer

November
Redcliff Hill: St Mary Redcliff Vestry puts
Georgian house, No. 51, under threat
University exhibits moon dust samples
(Apollo spacecraft landed on moon 21st
July)
Park Row: No. 32, Georgian birthplace of
University College, dem.
Sheene Rd/Malago Rd widened
Temple Gate: Terminus Hotel dem.
St James' Barton: pedestrian shopping
precinct opens
Centre: erection of new Demerara figurehead
Kingsweston House: 36 missing paintings
located, 3 in private offices
Colour TV programmes broadcast

December
Docks: Town Meeting in Colston Hall passes
a motion from the platform to abandon the
Parliamentary Bill
Essex St/Catherine Mead St: Dean Lane Pit/
East St railway embankment removed
East St to Malago Rd: new road opened

1970

January
Henbury Conservation Area designated (1st
of 29 under 1967 Civic Amenities Act)
John St/Nelson St/Tower Lane site: standing
buildings dem.
Cheltenham Rd: No. 176, Georgian house,
dem.
Broadmead/Union St: chemist corner-shop
for 150 years vacated
Passage Rd/Shipley Rd corner: old police
station dem.
ACBH discuss retaining gas lighting in one
part of city
Housing Act 1964: discretionary grants for
house improvements & flatting increased
to £1,000 & £1,200 resp. for 30-yr life
Kingsweston, The Echo: compiler campaigns
to stop Univ. of Bath's application to dem.
Vanbrugh's garden building

February

Paul St, Kingsdown, closed for construction
  of High Kingsdown
Redcliff Hill subway opens
Rupert St north side dem.
Bridge St closed for underground services
Parkway/Muller Rd roundabout opens
Redland Park Hall dem. for supermarket
St Peter's Hospital site: castle wall found
Temple Gate: Art Nouveau Lloyds Bank
  dem.

March

Horfield Common: barn dem. for houses
Brislington Hill south side set back
St Barnabas, City Rd: tower dem.

April

Ritz Cinema mostly dem.
Colston Ave: Artichoke PH dem.
St Nicholas' Church: 1st exhibition open
St James' Barton: St James's School dem.
Local bye-law: dogs to be leashed
Parkway/Bell Hill: entry & exit roads
  completed

May

Bristol Development Plan approved
  threatening, amongst other things, Bush
  Warehouse (MoHLG declines to list)
Purdown: new GPO telephone mast erected
Horfield Rd widened adjacent hospital
  precinct
Temple St: half of remaining street &
  Dr White's almshouses dem.
Colston St/Colston Ave: large C19
  commercial block dem.

June

Castle St: steps to postern gate to Castle
  discovered on Regent Cinema site
Brislington Hill: footbridge erected
Christmas St/Nelson St: Wheatsheaf PH
  dem.

July

SS *Great Britain* returns to dry dock bearing
  Prince Philip & to 100,000-strong welcome
Haberfield St: multi-story car park open
Broad St/John St corner dem.
Redcliff Hill: Mullett's Garage dem.
Parkway: stage 1 opens
Rupert St/Christmas St: island building dem.
Henleaze Blind Asylum sold for house
  building

Ashton Pumping Station commissioned to
  carry sewage from Bedminster, Ashton,
  Highridge, Withywood & Hartcliffe into
  Southern Foulwater Interceptor. 3 inverted
  siphons proposed to reduce river & Float
  discharges to 14% capacity

August

High St: Rummer Inn entrance made
Lawrence Hill Station dem.
St Luke's Church, Bedminster, dem.
Knowle: Harrowdene Rd Methodist Church
  dem.
Dighton St: convent converted to flats
Chesterfield Hse, Henbury: lead stolen, put
  at risk
Arno's Court Stables: left hand wall dem.
  without consent
Kingsweston House: Police HQ mooted.
  Results in attempt to overdevelop the park
  as regional HQ

September

Stoke Bishop: Kewstoke Rd made cul-de-sac
  at Jubilee fountain
Inns Court: 1st Bristol pre-fabs dem.
Fishponds Rd: railway bridge dem.
Clifton Bridge Station dem.

October

Redland Hill/Blackboy Hill roundabout:
  cottages dem.
Dustmen's strike produces rubbish heaps on
  The Downs etc.
The Centre: Bus Company's offices painted
  bright colours
St Raphael's Almshouses dem.

November

Redcliff Pde: Redcliff School dem.

December

Redcliff Hill: only one shop still open
Canford Lane: Coombe House dem.
Old Market St north side, adjoining Lower
  Castle St, dem.
Hartcliffe project: W D & H O Wills works
  starts on site

1971

January

Colston Ave: Atlas & Sun Buildings dem.
Parson St Station dem.
Royal Fort: Repton's Luccombe Oak
  felled

February

Portway: 1927 tennis courts removed
The Ridgeway: No. 4, Connell, Ward &
  Lucas 1935 house, restored
Lewin's Mead Chapel: City Cultural
  Committee twice refuses to meet CPAB over
  future of chapel
Decimal day

March

Haymarket: underground conveniences
  filled-in
Henleaze Rd: Blind Asylum dem.
Redcliff Way: railway viaduct dem.
Avon Way: Druid's Wood flats built in
  valley
Undertaking given to replace 3000 pre-fabs
  by 1976
Barrow Rd closed as the Queen's highway

April

Victoria St/Temple St corner dem.
Temple Church timber-framed rectory dem.
Clarence Rd, St Philip's: C17 Rose Harris
  flower shop dem.
Jacob's Wells Rd/Hotwell Rd: roundabout
  laid down
Rownham Hill improved
Coldharbour Farm Polytechnic: roads &
  foundations laid
Brislington Sq.: Georgian building housing
  Post Office dem.
University Walk closed as the Queen's
  highway
Stokes Croft: former Baptist College dem.
  appl. goes to DoE
Temple Meads: GWR offices (Brunel &
  Pope) dem. appl. by BR
Chapel Lane, Lawrence Weston: Church Hse
  at risk of dem. for City Housing
  development
Penlea House, Shirehampton: application for
  dem.
The White Horse PH, W-o-T: application for
  dem. Listed 1977 and partly dem. when

extended *c.* 1986
Brunel Technical College formed

May

Avon Gorge inquiry: 8-storey hotel called in
  after outline consent granted. Decision in
  Oct. – consent rescinded
Ashton Gate: restoration of turnpike
Rupert St: Frome culvert opened for
  strengthening
Don John Cross: lost for 3 days
Bath St closed as the Queen's highway

June

Broad Weir: Castle wall dem.
Westbury College: old people's flats erected
SS *Great Britain*: 11 trees gifted for masts
  and bowsprit
Charlotte St: John Laing threaten dem. of
  J R Phillips' Warehouse. Demolished
  March '72

August

Ashton Court: Architectural competition for
  reuse
Haymarket: Morley statue moved a few feet
M5: Avonmouth Rd spanned
Eastville Methodist Church closed
Parkway Methodist Church opened

September

CPAB sets up listing committee
Redland Railway Station: proposal to dem.
Henbury: C H Pearce propose to dem.
  Repton's Severn House
Dighton Court [**12/150**] dem.
Broadmead: proposal to pedestrianise
Colston Ave: MacAlpine's speculative
  Colston Centre, reaches 7th floor
Courage & Watney swap 68 public houses
Old Market: last Pie Poudre Court ceremony
Bathurst Hotel & Regency houses adjacent
  at risk of dem.
Dodo: *Architectural Design* carries J Hicks'
  lambast of planning

October

Police mounted section moves to new
  base at Bower Ashton
Campbells: last passenger trip & end of
  regular W-s-M/Wales service
Brislington: tram depot/garage closed
St Mark's Chapel: last visit of the Assize
  Judge
Parkway: Newfoundland Rd & Muller Rd
  works in progress

St George: Museum acquires tram depot
[**6/196**]
Royate Hill widened
Lawrence Weston: church house [**16/29**]
dem.
Blaise Hamlet: Oak Cottage to be thatched
Orpheus Cinema, Henleaze, closed for
supermarket conversion
Common Market entry voted by both
Commons and Lords

November

Upper Maudlin St: Moravian Church &
Church Lads Brigade HQ dem. for
hospital development
Arno's Court: wall being set back for road
widening
City Docks: Sir Hugh Casson commissioned
to report
Outer Circuit Rd: details publ.; 550 houses
compulsorily purchased at total
construction cost of £13m with 75% grant
from DoE

December

City Archivist, Miss E. Ralph, retires for
3rd holder of office
Upper Maudlin St: Moravian graveyard to
be cleared for hospital car park
Falcondale Rd: 3rd set of traffic lights
installed
Broad St: fire at Horts
Guildhall: Tolzey Court ends
Parkway: Baptist Mills Wesleyan Chapel
dem.
M4: Swindon–Maidenhead stretch opens
Kingswood: Hanham Rd/High St corner
dem.
Redcliff Hill: last shop closes

1972

January

Theatre Royal re-opens
Pembroke Rd/Downs: gallows tree felled
Southwell St closed
John St: Whitby's (formerly Ed. Everard
printing wks) to close
M4: Greyhound coach service to London
Victoria in 2½ hours
Bishop's Knoll sold for £275,000
Old Market St: No. 59 restored
Bristol Assizes & Quarter Sessions
superseded by Crown Courts

Castle St: Museum & Art Gallery
abandoned; multiple locations in lieu
'Blueprint for Survival' edition of *The
Ecologist* publishes sustainable growth
manifesto

February

Victoria St: Nos 33–39 (Rowe's and Iron &
Marble warehouses) dem.
John Totterdill ARIBA dies
St Peter's Church: nave, tower & chancel to
be stabilised as ruin
City Engineer, Mr James Bennett, retires
Rupert St re-opens
Colston Ave: Colston Centre attains 17
storeys
Newfoundland Rd closed for Parkway
construction
No-parking zig-zags laid down at pedestrian
crossings
Stokes Croft: Nos 78 & 80, Old Baptist
College, dem.
Cedar Hall, Frenchay: conversion starts.
Largely dem. in conversion & delisted at
compiler's request 1987
Alma Rd: fears for dem. of part of terrace in
connection with development of coalyard
(public inquiry 1974)
Power cuts for three weeks

March

High Cross architectural competition: winner,
Jon Catalani, with pavement in
St Peter's. Not executed
St George's Rd: soil investigation in horse
market behind Gt Western Hotel (now
Brunel House)
Canynge Sq. rejects new stubby lanterns on
lamp-posts
Broadmead: pedestrianisation proposals
publ.
Lower Ashley Rd: Onions & Skuse dem.
Queen Charlotte St: Windsor Castle PH dem.
Bus location laser plates set up

April

The Glorious Glosters march through the
city
Parkway: fire; part closed for six months

May

Fishponds Rd: No. 100 dem.
Old Market St: Nos 36–40 dem. commences
& is halted
Blackboy Hill: roundabout reduced

Portbury: West Dock inaugurated (cost
£13.8 million)
Parkway railway station opens
Death of Edward VIII

June

Old Market St: DoE asks Bristol Municipal
Charities to stop dem. of Nos 36–40
Orpheus Cinema dem.
Esso Hotel opens
Bath Rd: central reservation laid down at
Arno's Court
Lower Ashley Rd/Pennywell Rd: detour for
M32 construction
Westbury-on-Trym Conservation Area
designated
Falcondale Rd/Stoke Lane: traffic lights
installed

July

Wells Rd/Broad Walk: cleared for shopping
centre
Telephone Ave: telephone exchange dem.
Baldwin St: Scottish Widows' building dem.
Victoria St: Brown Bros dem.
Mitchell Lane and part of St Thomas St dem.
Blackboy Hill: Selman's remove 'by royal
appointment' inscrip. [16/146]
Clifton Down: railway station road closed

August

Stapleton & Frome Valley and City &
Queen Sq. Conservation Areas designated
Whitehall Rd/Chalks Rd widened
Lawrence Hill: large new roundabout
Armoury Sq.: centre house with Colston
bust dem. Later discovered that bust is by
Rysbrack [12/131]
Lower Ashley Rd: oldest pillarbox removed
[12/170]
HMS *Flying Fox* est. in Winterstoke Rd
Brandon Steep: Brandon Cottage saved
from dem. Overdeveloped by Bristol
Preservation Trust 1988
Hanham Mount: Messrs Wimpey lose their
appeal against refusal to build houses round
the mount

September

Clifton Conservation Area designated
Guinea St: No. 10 restored and painted
Purdown: old post office tower dem.
Netham: embankment mainly removed
St George's Rd: Central College (formerly
Fuller's carriage works) dem.

Old Market: early Guernsey letter box set up
on Mercury Hse

October

Prince St: art gallery proposed in Bush
warehouse. CWS clock tower dem.
Severnside: 15 ft whale washed ashore
City Docks: compiler initially chairs Fusion
Docks Study

November

Brunswick Sq.: Sec. of State disallows dem.
of Nos 1–6, but facadism scheme
nevertheless built
Corn St: pedestrianisation proposed
Temple St: fire station completed

December

Filton: Station Rd railway bridge widened
Broadmead: 'Jones of Bristol' bought out and
name lost
St Luke's School dem.
Arno's Vale Depot vacated by buses
Coombe Lane: Salisbury House dem.
[16/203]

1973

January

City Docks: Casson Study proposes
redevelopment of Redcliffe Backs, loss of
Bush Warehouse and Shakespeare etc.
Globe Cinema closed
M5 open from Portbury to Edithmead
Queen Charlotte St: facades only of Nos 53 &
55 saved
Bush Hotel closed
Bedminster Police Station to be vacated
Portland Chapel: alternative use as sports
hall suggested. Subsequently largely dem.

February

Highbury Chapel empty; may become a
warehouse
Whitfield Tabernacle, Kingswood: appl. to
dem. (public inquiry '84 prevents dem.)
Temple St Fire HQ moves in
Princess Victoria St: premises of Cowlins
facaded
Cart Lane dem.
Lewin's Mead: Garden Alley, C16/17
house dem. [18/45]

March

York Rd, Bedminster Bridge end: corner, probably incl. home of Hugh Owen [15], dem.

Three Lamps: fingerpost moved to Corporation's Dovercourt Rd yard and shops dem.

Stapleton Rd: accident results in toll house being dem.

Flying Fox taken to breaker's yard

St Luke's Rd: Victoria Park side dem.

Whitchurch Sports Centre opens

April

Dragonara Hotel opens

Park Place: Georgian terrage of houses regularised & converted to offices; front boundary walls removed in process

Redland Rd: Post-war house with studio dem. for flats

Stapleton Rd/Fishponds Rd corner: Methodist Chapel dem. [6/106]

Victoria St: Temple Colston School dem.

Concorde: two miniature cinemas opened

May

Bush Hotel dem.

Pembroke St: Nos 13–19 dem. after listing

Park Row: Sundon House, home of University, at risk

CPAB listing committee meets DoE inspector

Lewin's Mead: C1 Roman watermill discovered

Arnolfini moves to Canon's Road

Prewett St: Georgian house dem. [18/188]

June

Kingsdown Conservation Area designated 3 yrs after Kingsdown Conservation Group had been formed to this end

All Saints' St: 4 miniature cinemas opened

White Tree roundabout reduced

Redcross St: Sir Thomas Lawrence birthplace facaded & swamped

Kingsweston Down: TV aerial erected

Vandyke Cinema becomes bingo hall

Westbury Motors (Pratt's) dem. for housing

Union St: James Phillips closed

Clifton RC Cathedral dedicated

Broad Quay: Nos 19–24 dem.

Holiday Inn Hotel opens

July

600th Charter celebrations – county status 1373. Charter crown on centre. Evening Post exhibition on The Downs

Easton Rd roundabout opens

1st bus-only traffic lane, in Cheltenham Rd

1st Pelican, beeping ped. crossings at Morley statue & Brentry

Blackboy Hill: one-way system set up at junction with The Downs

Three Lamps: 2 Georgian houses dem. just before Queen's visit

August

8th: 600th anniversary of Edward III charter

9th: Queen visits Cathedral & 600 exhibition; Duke's 2nd visit to SS *Great Britain*

Pro-Cathedral fittings auctioned

September

Gloucester Rd: Morgan's Corner (formerly Colmer's) closed

Henbury Golf Course: 3 tall trees felled for new access road [3/169]

First exhibition of Bristol School of Artists 1810–1840 at City Art Gallery

October

Temple Way: Lincoln's warehouse dem.

St John's Lane/St Luke's Rd: corner pub dem.

Oxford St, Totterdown: houses dem.

Prince of Wales receives freedom of Merchant Venturers & visits SS *Great Britain*

Kingswood: Odeon dem.

Queen's Ave: Magg's building dem.

Colston Ave: Colston Centre shops open

Victoria St/Cart Lane corner dem.

Portway: widened under Sea Walls

November

Globe Cinema dem.

St Thomas' Church cleaned

Orpheus, Henleaze: 3 studio cinemas open

Broadmead pedestrianised

The Grove, west of Grove Ave, dem.

Redcliff Pde cleaned

Whitehall/Chalks Rd junction widened

Power engineers' work-ban causes power cuts

December

White Tree: diseased and felled

Energy crisis: shop lighting restricted

Kingswood: 'Mr Grace's surgery' dem.

Lewin's Mead Chapel, pre-Reformation remains of St Bart.'s & C17 buildings of Bristol Grammar School under threat of dem.

Portland Sq.: Nos 1–4, 5 & 6 under threat of facading (only No. 4 had original interior). In 1987 No. 6 was stripped of its joinery without consent with the benefit of £40,000 grant

c. 1973 Sneed Park: Bishop's Knoll & Towerleaze dem.

1974

January

Local Govt Re-organisation: Avon CC takes over strategic planning, highways, education for new county incl. Bristol; City of Bristol now a district council. Avon CC takes lease on spec. office block in St James' Barton

Hartcliffe: W D & H O Wills Head Office and Western Division completed at cost of £19.8m + plant to SOM & YRM design with manufacturing capacity of 350+ million cigarettes & 125,000 lbs hand-roll tobacco per week. Closure announced 1990

Holiday Inn Europa Double Studio cinema opens

King St, Seamen's Almshouses: paved court grubbed up, gentrified with walls & railings

February

West Town Lane: railway bridge dem.

Netham: traffic lights installed

Kings Weston Stables: Avon County tarmacs setts without consent

March

Worrall Rd, school site: start of dem.

Broad Walk: shopping centre opens

Centre: new public conveniences under Colston Centre open

Prince's Lane: Grand Spa ballroom closed; hotel to be sold

St Paul's St, Pritchard St & Norfolk Ave widening scheme. Dem. in Pembroke St, Gloucester St, Pritchard St & 21–31 Cumberland St. Rearguard action to save facades

General election results in Labour minority taking office

April

Netham: 2nd Bailey-type bridge over Feeder canal opens

Lewin's Mead, Garden Alley: old house dem.

Jamaica St: City Temple extension completed

May

Redcliff Way: Caxton House opens

Kings Weston House: paintings returned to entrance hall

Temple Way: Spear Bros, as far as Avon St, dem.

M5: Avonmouth bridge opens (one lane north & south)

Prince St: Bush warehouse (formerly Acramans) gutted, roof raised, converted to offices and Arnolfini

Odeon converted to 3 studio cinemas

Threats to: St Vincent's Hill Cottages; Scala Cinema; Pineapple Inn, St George's Rd; Alma Rd terrace

Kingsdown: annual Street Fair commenced to celebrate Conservation Area designation

June

Portland Sq. Conservation Area designated

Victoria St: spec. offices junction with St Thomas St squatted

St George's Park: lake floods houses

City Museum: basement store opened to public

Portway: dual carriageway under Sea Walls completed

Concorde: flies Boston–Paris–Boston in one day

July

Grosvenor Rd/Ashley Rd: triangle of properties dem.

Parkway/Newfoundland Rd roundabout: access to Newfoundland Rd opens

Hotwell Rd/flyover: corner properties dem.

Ashton Court: restoration & partial dem.

Portway closed: risk of rock falls

Rupert St: Crown & Dove PH closed

September

Queen's Rd: Brights becomes Dingles

Severe gales damage trees etc.

Prince St: CWS doorway statues placed with Museum

Temple Way: Bristol United Press occupies new premises

Hartcliffe/Airport Rd: dual carriageway opens

October

HMS *Bristol* receives freedom of city

Wapping Rd east side dem.

Bristol Omnibus Co. centenary: open day
with privately owned buses
Temple Gate: pedestrian footbridge erected
(£90,000)
Stoke Rd/Reservoir Rd: bus lane laid down
Scala Cinema closed
Totterdown, Wells Rd: above YMCA further
dem.
Blackboy Hill: No right turns

November

St Michael's Hill & Christmas Steps
Conservation Area designated
Pill Ferry ceases operation
Cotham Hill/Homoeopathic Hospital:
mini-roundabout
Blackboy Hill: NatWest Bank takes spec.
offices as regional HQ
Westbury-on-Trym: village hall (Crisp 1869)
re-opens
Prince St: CWS end of 2-year dem.
Keynsham: Charlton Cinema closed
Freeland Place, Hotwells: to be cul-de-sac
Old Market St: No. 92, Chequers PH,
threatened
Temple St: King's Head PH threatened
Scala Cinema dev.: Ombudsman advised
revised application not notified; Council
found guilty of maladministration in March
'75
Corn St: No. 35 facadism proposal by
NatWest Bank

December

Parkway/Newfoundland Rd roundabout:
access to Mina Rd open
The Centre: public conveniences dem.
Clifton Suspension Bridge: toll collection
automated
Brunswick Sq. cemetery: Latimer's grave
preserved
Eastville tram depot dem.
Stokes Croft: Hamilton House completed
Park St: Dixon's shop bombed
c. 1974 Avonmouth Congregation Church
dem.

1975

January

Whiteladies Rd: No. 149 dem. for offices
Redcliffe Church: Phoenix Assurance
restores & displays fire-engine
Berkeley Cafe for sale

Frenchay Pk Rd/Broom Hill corner widened
Southmead Rd north end widened

February

Park St & Brandon Hill Conservation Area
designated
Nelson St: new magistrates courts in use
Clifton Down/Clifton Down Rd: mini-
roundabout
Greystoke Ave: Concorde Drive built on line
of ring road
Mrs M Thatcher elected leader of
Conservative party

March

The Centre: new 'phone boxes and Burke
statue moved
Avonmouth/Severnside exceeds acceptable
levels of pollution

April

Victoria St/Temple St: offices on nw corner
completed
Temple St: Mardon's building dem.
Quakers' Friars: memorial window to John
Totterdill ARIBA
Luccombe Hill: black flag hung in memory of
County of Bristol
Kingsdown Sports Centre opened

May

College Green Conservation Area designated
Parkway opened to Newfoundland Rd
Peter St/Church Lane: Melhuish's site
excavations reveal Jewish community
pre-1290
The Downs: circular road closed for blasting
under Sea Walls
SS *Great Britain*: Prince Philip's 3rd visit;
funnel uncovered
Hope Chapel: application to dem.
St Gabriel's Church, Easton: building
inspector declares it not dangerous

June

Pennywell Rd: Brecknell Dolman & Rogers
premises dem.
Bristol Maternity Hospital: Ricketts' 1818
obelisk to Princess Charlotte discovered by
F Greenacre

July

Outer Circuit Rd: £2½m spent on Stage 1
land acquisition & dem. of houses. Avon CC
budgets £14m for Stages 2 & 3

Shirehampton Conservation Area designated
Stoke Hill/Saville Rd: traffic lights installed
Cumberland St: Nos 19–31 to be dem. &
replicated (offices)
Wilder St: No. 25 application for partial dem.

August

J K Taylor becomes Debenhams
Maternity Hospital moved from The Downs
to St Michael's Hill
Last (?) factory hooter sounds at Brooks
St Gabriel's Church: 9 days after 21 days'
notice given, dem.

September

Portbury: West Dock watered to 45 ft for
70,000 ton vessels. Largest entrance dock
in UK
Filton: Polytechnic opens
St George: St George's Church last peals
Westbury-on-Trym: Chock Lane new high
pavement
Cross Elms Lane: new houses replace
pre-fabs
LUTS (Land Use Transportation Study)
published, proposes tolls
Speedwell Ave/Whitefield Ave corner: No.
191, cottage, dem.
St Paul's: part declared a Housing Action
Area
St Paul St: Nos 15–21, Sec. of State confirms
facades may be replicated; decay & partial
destruction making reconstruction
impossible
St Paul St & Pritchard St: Nos 2–16 & 1–7
resp. Inquiry decision: all fronts to St Paul
St could be saved. No internal recording
done & no plasterwork saved.
Bath St, Nos 6–18, & Victoria St, Nos 2 & 16:
Courage make dem. application. 1986
inquiry decision: partial dem. allowed on
dubious grounds

October

Bedminster Local Plan in preparation
Sunday milk delivery ends
Prince St: Arnolfini opens
J R Preston replaces L Steen as City Planning
Officer

November

Henleaze Rd/Southmead Rd corner widened

December

Westbury-on-Trym: Elmfield School for
Deaf, housing development

Henbury: Repton's Severn House burnt
Belmont Rd: Plaque on birthplace of Field
Marshall Slim on No. 72
Plant-a-Tree Campaign totals 200 privately-
funded plantings in 3 yrs
Narrow Quay: 32 trees planted
Bridgwater Rd: roundabout at King's Head
PH for CEGB HQ
European Architectural Heritage Year 1975:
Oct–Dec exhibition 5 awards to Bristol,
1 exceptional merit, 3 commendations
Sex Discrimination & Equal Pay Act

Masterpiece

by John W. Totterdill ARIBA

Lord Beeching has returned to I.C.I. having bequeathed his name to the vocabulary of ruthlessness. The dust of controversy is settling, but in the last year or so the rail traveller has been able to see all over England the results of his reign. This may mean that you cannot reach the nicer seaside towns except by bus, the most uncivilised form of public transport that exists. More often it means new rolling stock, new signalling and welded track, and everywhere builders at work on the stations.

The Railway Age produced a new form of architecture and a great deal of magnificent engineering. Much of this is now being spruced up, but inevitably much of it is becoming redundant. Including the original Bristol Temple Meads Station.

The Great Western Railway was a Bristol venture originated in 1832 and eventually completed between Bristol and London in 1841. As everyone knows the Engineer was I. K. Brunel, and his spirit broods over every mile. Prior to 1830 the railway companies did not consider their responsibilities to include the provision of amenities for passengers. During the next ten years, stations were generally simple sheds with parallel iron colonnades supporting simple wooden trusses. Birmingham Curzon Street (by Philip Hardwick, 1838) is the first "Classical" application of Architecture. Brunel, conscious that he was designing what he called "the greatest work in England", made his terminus the architectural climax of his railway, the grandest station yet built.[1]

Like Caesar's Gaul, the building is in three parts, offices and trainshed linked by an odd building in which the clerks work in a maze of match-boarded offices crammed among the roof trusses over the engines.[2] The main offices face the street, with the Board Room of the Bristol Directors, a fantastic castellated staircase, and a flat for the Station Superintendent. They wear a vaguely Tudor dress, intended to pay tribute to what Brunel conceived as the period of Bristol's greatest achievements. Today our minds, and hence our eyes, prefer the less rhetorical engineering structures behind. The unique roof of the trainshed is one of the wonders of England, with huge twin cantilevers all in timber, perched on iron arcades. The fake "hammerbeams" which have so misled the historians, are merely minor struts with decorative pendants. The form of the roof derives from the need to avoid lateral thrust, the trainshed being at first floor level and the loads carried vertically through the arcades and the stone outer walls. It is the first of the great single-span railway roofs, and the last of the great timber ones.

Temple Meads was greatly extended in 1867 and again in the 1930's. It is now contracting, leaving Brunel's building high and dry. The last train left the Old Station last June, and the Railways have no further use for it. What they do want is a new office block to rehouse their scattered empire.

But is it really necessary to replace the one with the other, as is suggested? The trainshed is in excellent condition and contains a great deal of floorspace. Demolition would be extraordinarily wasteful, to say the least. The office block is threatened by Corporation road-widening proposals, though no scheme has yet been published. There are many acres of railway land at and around Temple Meads and railway reorganisation must surely lead to great changes. Better access to the Station, better parcel offices, car parking, adjoining road proposals, physical links with the city centre, the future of the goods yards at Pylle Hill and St. Philip's Marsh, liner trains, the G.P.O. requirements and the future of the Cattle Market, all these are problems which are interconnected with the lack of office space. Passenger amenities today must surely include adequate links with other forms of transport, and the time has come to recreate Temple Meads as a Regional Communications Centre.[3]

The future of the Brunel building must be discussed in this context and not on its own. The historical and engineering arguments for preservation are strong, and perhaps also the sentimental. Engineers today are increasingly conscious of the importance of such early monuments of their profession. But the strongest claim is simply that it is there, that it would cost a great deal to demolish, and that already many uses have been suggested for its valuable floorspace. The trade exhibition hall which Bristol has long discussed, badly needs and certainly cannot afford, could yet be provided here. And where is there a more fitting home than Temple Meads, at the heart of a regional transport centre, for the transport museum of which the seeds have already been sown in the city. Why not, indeed, bring the Western Region's own excellent museum from Swindon to its logical home here?

But demolition or its alternative use are probably several years and several financial crises away. The immediate threat to Brunel appears to be conversion to a temporary carpark, with all that that usually entails of hard usage and poor maintenance. It would be the beginning of the end. Almost any other temporary use would by better, or none at all. There is a strong case for purchase by the Corporation.

At Euston the Railways demolished a masterpiece only to find their plans so changed that demolition is now seen to have been unnecessary. The lesson is obvious. The Railways should look before they leap. The opportunities for all kinds of improvement at Temple Meads are immense, and urgent. If the wider view is taken, there is plenty of room for offices as well as Brunel. Bristolians will expect to see these wider problems discussed and answered before they are asked to consider the loss of such an asset as the famous shed. This building is much too important to become the victim of piecemeal decisions taken in the dark.

Published in *Journal 11*, Bristol Building and Design Centre, November 1965

Footnotes
1 Listed Grade I in 1966.
2 The engine shed with Brunel's drawing office over, the latter stripped of historic matchboarding, against the advice of the Victorian Society in 1988, ironically by the Exploratory.
3 An opportunity missed by the Planning Committee who consented to an enlarged, troglodyte bus centre, disparagingly referred to as the Badger sett, at St James' Barton in 1988.

KINGSDOWN

or

One Damned Georgian Building After Another

A CONTINUOUS TRAGEDY

Being the Phase 1 Battle & Featuring 146 Houses

The background, overtures, representations and promises, and their eventual setting aside in the battle for the lower slopes of Kingsdown, although referred to elsewhere, are not covered in detail. The process had started well beforehand but it was worked out on the ground in the early years of the 1963-1975 period. Reece Winstone had been secretary of the Civic Society at the time. This résumé was prepared by the compiler from newspaper articles and amenity society minutes for the post-war display he designed and mounted as part of the popular 1987 'Kingsdown 250' exhibition in the City Museum & Art Gallery. The heading comes from the exhibition, with apologies to SAVE. Maintenance costs may prove a twenty-year life sufficient for the high rise blocks and presumably in that eventuality a return to family dwellings may result, with the task of obtaining a new, green and convincing *genius loci*:

In 1956 the Medical Officer of Health surveyed properties in Kingsdown in connection with slum clearance as provided for in the Housing Act of the same year. It was later maintained that a prior decision had been made by the Housing Committee to clear the area . . .

Delays in making the survey findings public led to rumour, bringing forth letters and articles in the press putting the Corporation on notice that Kingsdown was 'Bristol's Montmartre' and a 'unique survival'.

The then *Western Daily Press* reporter, Tom Stoppard, wrote in December 1956: 'The traditionalists are right. The narrow streets – some little more than paths – offer a glimpse of a quieter contented world as they fall in cobbled slopes and worn steps, confined by mellow cottages with faded, intriguing windows.'

The residents, fearful of compulsory purchase, responded by forming the Kingsdown & St Michael's Area Protection Association. Its secretary published in the press a photograph of Portland House, Portland Street, boarded-up and vandalised following a closing order imposed two years previously, as an indicator of deliberate Corporation inaction.

In October 1957 the largest clearance areas in Bristol for many years were confirmed, affecting 4,312 people in Bedminster, St Philip's, Easton, Redfield, Lawrence Hill, St Paul's, Barton Hill, St George, Ashley Vale and Kingsdown. All the houses in the Order were declared to be unfit for human habitation. The chairman of the Housing Committee said that there were 10,000 houses that had to be cleared in five years and that the Committee was not doing this because of the Rent Act; they had a statutory obligation to deal with unfit properties. However, another Councillor said he had personally examined the exterior of the 111 Kingsdown houses included in the Order and his view was that perhaps 50% should not be demolished but restored – 'If you demolish 111 you will get some 500 more in decay'.

Ian Nairn of *Architectural Review* wrote in September 1957 on behalf of the Counter-Attack bureau: 'Kingsdown is one of the sights of Britain, let alone Bristol; nowhere else is there an 18th century suburb apparently hanging in mid-air over a big city; it is as though Hampstead rose up at the beginning of Baker Street. Here is a grand chance for the city to plan with its citizens, not against them.'

The Bristol Civic Society pronounced: 'We consider the domestic Georgian houses of Kingsdown provide unique groups of high architectural merit, and that every endeavour should be made to preserve them as an interesting, valuable and still useful amenity of Bristol. The gaps in the area caused by war damage or by unavoidable demolition of unfit property should be filled by new buildings most carefully designed to harmonise with the old.'

The Deputy Town Clerk promised that 'the Civic Society's views would be borne in mind'.

In the meantime Mr Bryan Little, writing in *Gloucestershire Countryside* in November 1957, asked that shabbiness should not be mistaken for neglect; some owners had spent money and Kingsdown was not universally bad. He thought 150 houses were beyond hope and what was needed was rehabilitation. 'Kingsdown's qualities make Chelsea look quite literally flat and with its precipitous charm it can give points to the most recherché roads of Hampstead.'

John Betjeman added: 'This airy suburb, this place of Georgian view-commanding terraces, trees, cobbled streets, garden walls and residential quiet, is all the more attractive for its unexpectedness so near the middle of Bristol. I hope that Bristol Corporation which has in its trust the most varied and, to me, the most beautiful large city in England, will spare Kingsdown. Such a unique district can never be replaced. It should, in the main, be reconditioned rather than torn down.'

Sir Albert Richardson PPRA wrote: '. . . once the most renowned residential suburb in the western region [he had written the then definitive book on the West Country Georgian]. 18th century Kingsdown belongs to the nation and if the principle is accepted that everything visual is common property, then the local authority should be held to account for their vandalism.'

The Protection Association brought in the Royal Fine Arts Commission who confirmed the 'great architectural interest of the area'. Later the Commission expressed their concern with an unwise turn of phrase merely 'regretting the need for such extensive demolition'. At that time anything smacking of semi-vernacular Georgian, precisely the merit of the Kingsdown lower slopes, was at risk. Even the formal King Square was by no means safe. So when RFAC declared it was not in a position to comment on new building design, things indeed looked black.

The Council for the Preservation of Ancient Bristol (formed in 1936 at the suggestion of the Kyrle Society to resist demolition of historic buildings) argued strongly for the best houses to be spared – 5 and 6 Blenheim Square and 1 Spring Hill – and that 'the general character of this most unusual and attractive district should most certainly be left unimpaired, particularly the almost unique cobbled and/or stepped streets (e.g. Spring Hill and Gay Street) . . . In a like manner, the various attractive groupings of houses should be respected even where none of them, individually, are in Grade I or II'.

It continued: 'The district, and the groups of houses within it, should be considered from the angle of civic planning and general amenity, and not merely from technical reports, house by house, on the condition of its individual buildings. From this it would follow that several ranges, e.g. Fremantle Place, Francis Place and perhaps Armada Place, should if possible be reconditioned as small residences, and not pulled down. [A statement made predicting the need for conservation area designations 9 years before the Bill.] . . . we would not oppose any of the demolitions proposed in the following: Dove Street, Thomas Street, Cox's Buildings, Princes Row, Dalton Square, Carolina Avenue and Row, and Bush Street . . . The following should certainly be kept and reconditioned: Duke Street, Blenheim Square, Spring Hill (below Dove Street).'

The CPAB also maintained that 'certain of the buildings in Hillgrove Street should be retained together with the stepped sidewalks in this street [which] should on no account be obliterated'.

Following the holding of a public meeting, to which the Civic Society and CPAB were not invited, the two bodies met the City Clerk, the Housing Manager and the then City Architect. It transpired that the Ministry of Housing had asked for the façades on the north side of King Square to be retained. It is also minuted that the council had decided 'as a matter of policy that no improvement grants should be made unless additional units of accommodation were to be provided'. The City Architect, like the City Clerk earlier, would 'have in mind the preservation of the more historic buildings and that it was not anticipated that any 10–12 storey construction would be erected, but in the main 4–5 storey'.

In December 1958 the Ministry of Housing called a public inquiry into '146 2, 3 and 4-storey Georgian houses as being unfit for human habitation and whether the best method of dealing with them is by demolition'.

Of these 28 were listed for their special architectural and historic interest, Grade II and III. One house had a demolition order pending and it was necessary to take 99 others for roads, etc.

The Deputy Planning Officer gave evidence that Blenheim Square was required for hospital zoning (he was referring to a maintenance shop) but that the Hospital and Planning Committee would, in exchange, take Area E out of the precinct (an undertaking apparently rescinded after demolition and which the authorities cannot explain to this day). It was proposed to 'interfere as little as possible with the existing road pattern', and to retain Montague Hill.

The new City Architect said that because many houses were in multiple occupation, it was not practical to achieve equal density houses of 2/3 storey to current standards. He had therefore designed flats and maisonettes of 3, 4 and 5 storeys.

Eleven months later the Minister confirmed the compulsory purchase and clearance orders with the exception of part of the north side of King Square and a part of Hillgrove Street. The inspector's report stressed that the buildings lacked the finer points of Georgian domestic architecture and that redevelopment should be to a greater density. The Minister's direction that the commercial properties in King Square (Nos 12–15) be included did not extend to the dwelling houses at Nos 8 and 9 (which the Protection Association and CPAB had pleaded be spared) as these could be seen to be simply a continuation of the condemned Duke Street.

Six months later the newly elected Conservative majority, for years in opposition, went to Whitehall to seek the Minister's agreement to deal with unfit properties on an individual basis, but he would have none of it.

In 1963 the City Architect cast aside all thought of preserving the historic buildings and street pattern and returned a scheme of three high rise slab blocks with medium rise cross ranges, designed in association with John Laing Construction Ltd.

INDEX OF PLACES

INDEX OF ARCHITECTS, ENGINEERS, SCULPTORS

Panoramas of the Period

†(1) *c.*1963: From above Stoney Hill south to the CWS building and Gaunts' House. The Georgian house was colourwashed orange.

(2) 4.00pm 18 April 1963: The eastern prospect of Clifton Heights, newly erected, to the escarpment of Lansdown. The remains of the Prince's Theatre hang on in Park Row, with the Georgian home of University College. Sir Geo. Oatley's University tower awaits his biographer. The size and proportion of the Robinson building in Victoria Street unleash the tower and podium form for corporate display.

*(4) September 1974: St James' Barton & Knowle from 74 Kingsdown Parade The liftcore of Castlemead House, spec. offices by Town & Commercial Hotels Ltd, a victim of the 1974 crash, completed 1981 after deliberate delays to avoid rates and 1/3rd unlet as late as 1986, makes an unwelcome addition just as did the serpentine York House, Barton House and Avon House North when the City encouraged redevelopment and gave consent in 1964 to demolish the remaining two sides [**64, 65**] of St James' Square which it had sold to the developer Copthall Holdings Ltd.

*(5) December 1974: Same vie three months later at nig

(3)   10.45 am 12 April 1963: The west end of the city looking north-west from the Robinson building before high-rise offices blighted St John's-on-the-Wall, off right, but the horizon is already impaired. St Nicholas still a shell.

(6)   4.00pm 17 August 1966: The southerly prospect of the Robinson building looking to Temple Meads. The 1870's Victoria St cut in process of redevelopment following blitz' damage, but without regard to historic intersections. The Iron & Marble Co.'s flat-iron, bottom centre, and Rowe Bros' HQ of *c.*1870 with good arcaded facade demolished for a spec. office block of dismal form by Mithras Properties in 1974 at Nos 35–49 Victoria St.

(7)   11.55am 16 Augu
1966: Looking north from t
cupola of the CWS HQ, Prin
Street Gaunts House for Pea
Assurance, 1953, the Ne
Entertainment Centre ar
Trenchard St car park all jar
the urban grain. Nos 2–
Colston St, a C19 flat-iron grou
in coloured brick, hang o

†(8)   31 May 1966: T
City looking east from Cab
Tower Nine churches w
Days Road gasomete
beyond, centre. Promine
chimneys in Netham. T
roofs of C18 warehouses
Gaunts Lane, demolish
1988, in front of Sir Ge
Oatley's Sun Buildings corn
of Clare St/Colston Ave. T
Entertainment Centre ste
frame erected bottom le

(9)   12.05pm 30 Augu
1964: From Myers multi-stor
car park to Rupert Stre
The Nelson Street site clear
for Nelson House, a spec. offi
development by Hollow
Developments 1967, and t
Police HQ & Magistrates' Cou
in the same yea

**(10)   10.45am 4 June
1962: The Horsefair, looking
west** from Lewis's roof
garden, now sadly defunct, to
the walled city left and Royal
Fort right. Centre shot is Lex
multi-storey car park, an early
hub to the inner circuit road in
Lewin's Mead. Below Royal
Fort Horfield Rd houses
extant, [114]. The University
development unduly
prominent atop the
escarpment.

**(11)   4.20pm 15 August
1966: Looking north from 12th
floor of Polden House flats on
Windmill Hill** Housing
demolished for industrial units
alongside Bedminster station,
awnings now removed. The
City Farm stepped into the
wasteland. One of the WD &
HO Wills buildings now
demolished and all the
chimneys taken down.

1963

Evening Post, Tuesday, March 26

Turnpike to come down under road improvement plan

One of Bristol's two surviving turnpike houses is to be demolished so that a road improvement scheme can be carried out in Bedminster.

It is Winford House, built more than 200 years ago at the junction of Parson Street and Bedminster Down to collect tolls from people travelling to Winford.

Four years ago it was in a derelict condition. Tramps used it for sleeping and children also played there.

Then a building firm, J. and R. Rooff, Ltd., became tenants and spent £2,000 on putting it in order.

Now, however, Bristol Corporation are buying the property from Mill and Rockleys, the owners, so that they can knock it down and introduce the one-way road system.

Mr Reece Winstone, Bristol photographer, is opposing the scheme. He claims that the "simple solution" of demolishing property on the corner of Bedminster Down Road and Winterstoke Road will come about by 1968 with, perhaps, a fly-over.

SENTENCE

He told the Evening Post today:

"Because this is expensive in 1963, the turnpike is under sentence of death. Who is going to put it back in 1968 when a proper road system is designed?

"The residents in the roads affected don't want A38 traffic passing their doors. And lovers of old Bristol will protest at the senseless destruction of another valuable piece of historic architecture."

But a Corporation spokesman said the Planning Committee reaffirmed as recently as February 6, their decision about the fate of the property, which is on the supplementary or secondary list of buildings of architectural or historic interest.

And a Mills and Rockley spokesman said: "While one regrets its passing, every Bristolian recognises that this is one of the worst bottlenecks in the city."

(12) 10.45am 14 December 1962: **Clearing the ruins of the medieval Bishop's Palace,** fired 1851 and finally demolished to provide a ready site for a school building – a tragic and avoidable loss symptomatic of the rest of the period. Originally the walling (like the rest of the rubblestone of the cathedral) would have been plastered externally [**11/59**].

(13) **11.30am 19 February 1963: St John's churchyard, Bedminster** Folorn remains of the font in an icy churchyard, perhaps from an earlier church, long before the possibility of the yard becoming a public open space graced with archaeological importance. After survey of 244 overgrown funerary monuments in 1974 and subsequent clearances, today the medieval cross is in dire state. [**25/44**]

(14) 7.30pm 11 June 1963: **Bedminster Down Road Turnpike** Opposition to the demolition of this fine classical example for road widening brought no co-operation from the City Engineer and alternatives were sought in vain. Pl. [**25/45**] shows there may have been a detached toll-booth too.

(15) 6.00 pm 12 April 1963: Little Castle Street C17 PH of listable quality contrasts with the new mood.

(16) 12.00 noon 13 September 1963: The Regent Theatre, Castle Street One of the few buildings to survive the blitz' in the central shopping area, perhaps on account of its concrete construction. Here seen at the start of demolition. St Mary-le-Port tower under repair. Castle moat, foreground.

(17) 2.45pm 23 March 1963: 106 & 104 Stokes Croft E W Godwin's surviving Bristol masterpiece of 1862, listed in 1966 grade II*, in its original setting alongside a Georgian pair damaged but not terminally so by the outward spread of shopkeeping. Successor of this pair, Westmoreland House 1966, purpose-designed for the defunct Regional Pool Promotions, blighted the whole block and the present-day conservation area, including another listed Georgian house, just extant today, around the corner in Ashley Road. Meanwhile 104, today in the 'at risk' category, rots, recently burnt.

(18) 11.15am 21 July 1963: Redland Hill House, c.1750 by James Bridges with its lime plaster hanging off and railed garden wall. One of the first semi-detached houses, one semi demolished in 1933, a speculation by the owner of Redland Court who did not stint on the Gibbs window surrounds. Listed in 1959; do the railings survive?

(19)   7.05pm 1 May 1963: Narrow Quay Arguably the most historic backdrop to the city docks to survive into the 1960's. A rich mix of buildings waterfronted the Georgian merchants' houses in Prince Street. Only the right-hand section survives today. The CWS had already speculated with office development, left, foreseeing sale and demolition of the Edwardian HQ.

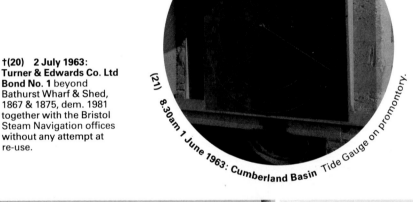

†**(20)   2 July 1963: Turner & Edwards Co. Ltd Bond No. 1** beyond Bathurst Wharf & Shed, 1867 & 1875, dem. 1981 together with the Bristol Steam Navigation offices without any attempt at re-use.

(21)   8.30am 1 June 1963: Cumberland Basin Tide Gauge on promontory.

†**(22)   1963: The Western Counties Agricultural Co-operative Association Limited** offices of 1897 and their mill of similar date beyond the 1863 Hide (now Severn) shed (left) and lighterage of concrete and steel. Why did the mill and adjacent warehouse go?

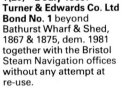

**(23)   11.20am
24 February 1963: A treed
Hotwell Road** at junction
with Granby Hill. Drinking
fountain 1902 erected in
memory of Simon Short
overlooked the lock. [See
31/92 for story.] Removed to
corner of Hotwell Road and
Merchants Road in July
1966. Cumberland Hall left
centre and C19 houses left
demolished for road
widening.

**(24)   11.10am
24 February 1963: Hotwells**
Classical repose of the
ladies' waiting room,
presumably demolished in
connection with the
Cumberland Basin scheme.
Monogram to left is RSA;
that to right appears to read
1893. Suggestions please for
exact location.

**(25)   8.15am 1 June
1963: Cumberland Basin**
Harbour Master's house of
1858 before demolition in
July 1964 in connection with
new swing bridge, with
Rownham House, dower
house of Ashton Court
emparked distant, to suffer
similarly. The clock appears
to confirm the
photographer's diary entry
[**31/263**].

(26) 11.30am 31 May 1963: Prince Street Farrs Lane to Assembly Rooms Lane. Sites in institutional uses beyond the row of five merchants' houses seen prior to demolition of the whole block for the Unicorn Hotel and car park. See pl. [19] for the rear frontages to Narrow Quay.

(28) 12.10pm 5 November 1963: Feeder Road railway bridge propped prior to widening of abutments. A motorised barge passes.

(27) 9.50am 27 March 1963: The Georgian turnpike house, Feeder Road Subsequently or separately left, the lock-keeper's house.
Demolished shortly afterwards: the site remains empty. Presumably the buildings were simply seen as an encumbrance.

(29) 11.00am 22 May 1963: Narrow Quay to Prince's Wharf MV *Benfleet*, built Holland 1907, bought by Fred. Ashmead & Son *c.*1930. 3-ton electric travelling cranes nos 29–31 1949 by Stothert & Pitt designed to service the largest visiting cargo ship, MV *Boston City*. Crane 32 right added in 1950, 10-ton capacity. All four saved from the scrap heap by City Docks Ventures Ltd in 1978.

**(30)   10.05am
12   April   1963:
Whiteladies Gate**
Clifton   Down
Station and the
coal yard, entered
left,   lay   behind
D & E shoe repairs
sharing a site that
had been a nursery
since the Regency.

**(33   &   34)
9.50   &   9.55am
19   July   1963:
28–32 Bedminster
Parade   to   Boot
Lane**   "Wixon's
Kink" as No. 30
was   to   become
known on account
of   the   20-year
resistance of the
owners of this infill
property   to   road
widening and the
desultory   offer   of
compensation.
'They Can't Close
Us Down . . .'
[**31/170**].

**(31)   11.05am
8   November   1963:
Site of St John's Bridge
from Christmas Street**
C19 buildings left and
right   dem.   for   inner
circuit   road.   Most
interesting are the C18(?)
warehouses with hipped
roofs distant on site of
Greyfriars spec. office
development   for
Howard   Farrow
Developments 1974.

**(32)   11.20am 21 July
1963: 41–45 Corn Street,
5-bay Italian palazzo** as
commercial architecture;
Royal   Exchange
Buildings replaced with
a crass speculation for
Debenham, Tewson &
Chinnocks in 1966 which
did real damage to one
of Bristol's best streets.

**(35)   11.25am
25   October   1963:
131   North   Street,
Bedminster**   Arthur
Baker's closing down
sale. He had bought
Winstone & Son, out-
fitters of East Street
before the war, as Reece
became   a   full   time
freelance photographer.

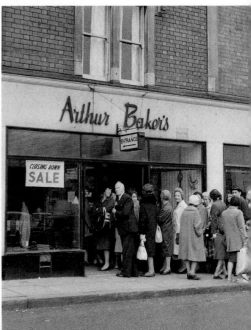

(41, 42 & 43) 11.40am 31 May 1963: Little Theatre, Colston Street Last performance of The Rapier Players in *Rock-A-Bye Sailor.* Gas mantles up the entrance stairs went with the gallery when the auditorium was ramped.

(37) 7.00pm 11 June 1963: 84–87 Old Market Street C18 and C17 houses between Temple Way and Church Lane. Right Bristol Co-operative Chemists & Advertising Dept in post-war office building.

(36) 7.05pm 11 June 1963: Old Market Street from Carey's Lane Nos 75–79, an C18 & C19 row demolished for Temple Way underpass, leaving the side of the Stag & Hounds PH exposed, the subject of chronic attempts at facelifting and ill-conceived internal alterations in 1987. The same year the Loyal Order of Ancient Shepherds' C17 timber-framed house immediately beyond suffered similarly, despite intervention by the SPAB.

(38) Far left: 11.40am 8 November 1963: Passage Street looking to Counterslip Old buildings hang on in Temple Back above the roof of the Central Electric Generating Station, left. The cold stores in Queen Street demolished for redevelopment which removed the sheer wall character facing the Float. The former tramway generating station by W C Green of 1899, grade II, converted to offices by Courages in 1986 with visibly inserted floors and without reinstatement of the parapet.

(39) 10.20am 19 July 1963: 2, 3, 4 & 8 Tower Hill with Central Health Clinic by Dening, a fine inter-war building presently at risk from redevelopment, with C19 St Philip & St Jacob church hall rising in front in Marybush Lane.

(40) 10.40am 20 July 1963: Tower Hill Prince of Wales PH right faces Poeton Industrial Plating Co., demolished for Central Ambulance Station. Shops and offices in Lower Castle St were short-lived. The traffic flow is reversed today.

(44 & 45) 18 September 1963: The Empire Theatre, Carey's Lane Midday on the day before the sale of fittings – including a large number of bicycle tyres! Apparently polished columns to bow fronted boxes, Moorish brickwork externally [**31/10**].

(46) 10.00am 27 March 1963: Carey's Lane, Old Market Last week of The Tatler 'continental cinema', so named 1947, formerly the Olympia Cinema of 1912 taken from under the canopy of the Empire Theatre. Closes 30 March, fittings sold September, demolished January 1965. [**31/3**].

†(47,
†48, *49
*50) 1963:
Ashton Court
Kitchen Court clock.
Bell over C16 wing dem.
as was the winter garden
c.1963. The still shambolic
Gothick wing sadly resashed.
The Huntsman's Hall
Gothick chimney-
piece before a
partition wall
was whammed
in.

(51)   9.35am 15 July 1963: 13 St Thomas Street, Kingsdown C19 off-licence; last licensee Gilbert William Shearn and the scene of a murder. Dalton Square distant left. Demolished under compulsory purchase powers for council housing.

(52)   4.30pm 23 August 1963: Albion Road, Lower Easton 25 early C19 houses demolished to form open space put to no obvious purpose, save a small play-ground in left distance. The fine CWS works dept, unlisted, burnt 1989, but capable of reconstruction. St Mark's, distant, the subject of a damaging conversion to flats by Bristol Churches Housing Association in 1989 and unbecoming support from the Bishop of Bristol when it seemed possible the protesting amenity society might turn the planning committee decision.

(53)   4.40pm 23 August 1963: Albion Road, Lower Easton Taking the air on the front step of a house seen in [**52**].

(54)   10.25am 15 August 1963: Roman Road, Lower Easton Left, rear of a row seen in [**52**].

(55)   10.00am 25 November 1963: Homefield House, St George A Georgian house with *claire-voie,* home of a local poet at side of Harvey's Lane. The quiet rural landscape now overrun with poorly designed elderly persons' dwellings.

(56) 1.00pm 5 November 1963: Southmead Road/ Wellington Hill West before removal of trees for speculative housing. The iron finger post *Gloucester* a casualty of progress.

(57) 10.25am 7 July 1963: Hollywood House, Cribbs Causeway T planned alignment of M5 divorced this entry and C19 lodge from t late-Georgian mansion, home of the late Sir George White. Fortunately t best part, the gates and piers, was set up beyond M5.

(58) 10.45am 25 November 1963: Cleve Dale, Downend A C17 or earlier house, extended in the Regency period, seen before demolition, to which possibly the Wrightian barn in Overndale Road belonged.

†(59) 1963: High Street Shirehampton Barn of unknown date before conversion with estate offices of Kings Weston House beyond, before demolition of latter.

†(60) 1963: High Street Shirehampton Arts and Crafts estate offices in course of demolition for a filling station. The row of triple bows made particularly good townscape.

†(61) 1963: The Green, Shirehampton Four Georgian houses demolished for a row of unseemly shops shortly after this was taken.

(62) 11.40am 24 February 1963: Eastwood Farm, Brislington in its mid-C20 setting prior to council purchase of two outbuildings and farmland for refuse tipping and planned landscaping to form public open space. The ring road crossing planned for the 1990's off right. The best possible use for this listed house is as a private dwelling, not as a 'leisure facility'.

(63) 11.50am 24 February 1963: Eastwood Farm, Brislington C17 house with good plasterwork, then as now in need of conservative repair.

1964

Evening Post, Tuesday, September 15

St James Square

Re the proposed development of the area bounded by Cumberland Street and Bond Street by Copthall Holdings Ltd.

May we Bristol-lovers have an assurance that St James Square (which is within the area) will be left untouched?

Readers will recall the struggle to save the delightful Georgian Houses, with their unique shell porches: how, by bending the line of the future arterial road on the map, this characteristic area of our old city was preserved in the late 1940's.

I therefore ask: Is St James Square safe for posterity?

REECE WINSTONE

(64 & 65) 11.30am 30 August 1964: St James' Square Bristol's second Georgian square relieved of two of its sides [27/122–6]. Roydon House home of the director of Baptist Mills spelter bereft of its modillion cornice and Westhill's (Factors) of its centre pediment.

Evening Post, Tuesday, December 15

They fight to save a city's relics

Bristol Archaeological Committee should not exist. Its secretary, Mr Reece Winstone, says so.

And if Bristol Corporation were more concerned with preserving the city's history, it would not exist.

"But they seem to have no consciousness of the importance of preservation," claims Mr Winstone. . . .

The eight-year-old committee is the watchdog of Bristol's historical monuments. Its members are more concerned with small landmarks, statues and signs, common centuries ago but fast becoming unique, than with large buildings. . . . The work of Bristol Archaeological Committee is centred

within the city boundaries. Its formation in 1956 linked together the Bristol and Gloucestershire Archaeological Society, which covers the county, and the Council for the Preservation of Ancient Bristol, which deals mainly with larger buildings.

Its members include local historians, a couple of active archaeologists and the city archivist, under the chairmanship of museum director Mr Alan Warhurst, who took over a few months ago on the death of historian Mr Frederick Jones. . . .

Often the committee wins. Like the time they insisted the old town wall should remain when a new block of offices was built on the site in Baldwin Street. The planners bowed down – and the block was built round the wall leaving access for anyone who wanted to see it. . . . They want to save the last Severn Trow, the 130-year-old river

barge lying almost derelict at Avonside Wharf. It will cost about £7,000 to buy it and exhibit it at the museum and the committee hasn't that sort of money. . . .

What Bristol Archaeological Committee can and is determined to do is save as much historically interesting material as possible from oblivion.

At Redcliffe, the Corporation has a yard where the more unusual remains of demolitions are stored.

"The stuff is just left there to rust and fall to bits," said Mr Winstone. "Yet there are street signs and road stones and some quite unique specimens there which should be replaced in some prominent position. The only thing that seems to be of any use are Victorian lamp-posts. . . . The council are making them electric and using them in King Street and Christmas Steps."

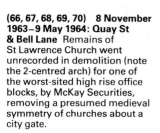

(66, 67, 68, 69, 70) 8 November 1963–9 May 1964: Quay St & Bell Lane Remains of St Lawrence Church went unrecorded in demolition (note the 2-centred arch) for one of the worst-sited high rise office blocks, by McKay Securities, removing a presumed medieval symmetry of churches about a city gate.

(71, 72) 7 April, 30 May 1964: Deanery Road Mission Hall of 1887, Folk House 1920 onwards. Roof damaged in the blitz and demolished for a library extension of much less vigour. Council have declined suggestions this year to reopen Lower Lamb St viaduct to pedestrians.

(73) 11.15am 11 December 1964: Dean Lane, St Paul's Parochial School in demolition. 1880's Gothic Revival shaved to austerity.

†(74) c.1964: Newfoundland St Chapel? Confirmation of this location for this 1850's frontage invited from readers.

*(75) February 1964:
Christopher Thomas & Bros
Soapworks, Broad Plain, later
Gardiners who removed the
merlons. Architect possibly
C. Jones, 1881, said to be
inspired by a visit to Florence
and fortunately listed.

*(76) February 1964:
Bathurst Parade, Warriner's
Warehouse Another Italianate
or Moorish design *c.*1865,
possibly Gingell & Lysaght.
Listed, but this did not prevent
the removal of the iron hopper
lights with consent in 1988.

(77) 3.45pm 9 May 1964:
All Saints Lane Demolition of
Fry's No. 7 Factory of 1905
[**32/146**] for Capital &
Counties' dreadful Pithay
House office block.

†(78 & 79) February 1964:
Tower Lane & Nelson St
Terracotta at base of Fry's No.
7 entrance rotunda. Town &
City Properties' equal eyesore,
Tower House, to rise in
foreground.

(80) 11.20am 20 October
1964: Bridge St Meanwhile
the Georgian survivors of
Bridge St were also
demolished.

(81) 3.35pm 7 April 1964: Temple St and Water Lane A blitzed red and buff brick Cashmore & Co. of 1870's faces the Cornubia. Temple Almshouses beyond right. Only the Cornubia remains.

(82) 3.30pm 7 April 1964: Victoria St/Cart Lane Fine homogeneous commercial street architecture of the 1870's bowed but confident. Now entirely demolished.

(83) 10.15am 31 August 1964: West side of Victoria St Centre No. 139 Abraham Levy glass importer, right of Catholic Schools (truncated?). Typical of the ashlar and brick mix of commercial facades of the 1870's.

(84) 10.25am 31 August 1964: Victoria St/Temple St The 1870's flat-iron of coloured brick under cement dem. 1986 (?) for roadway.

(85 & 86) 11.50am 8 March 1964: Victoria St with H Crisp's Bristol Carriage Works of 1870's [**8/27**]. A closer view of its logical decorative scheme, right, shows up its less competent neighbour [**31/159**].

Bottom left: (87 & 88) August & October 1964: Victoria St demolitions Corner block centre left by J Michelen Rogers (c.f. No. 16 Vic. St, extant) reduced to two storeys.

89) 3.30pm 7 April 1964: St Thomas t Homely commercial stuff on corner of Mitchell Lane.

†(90) 1964: 14 Redcliff Street If Victoria St had uniformity, Redcliff St, then still a considerable and historic thoroughfare, boasted this magnificent dark pink sandstone *palazzo*, deeply moulded and carved, commissioned by WD & HO Wills of Foster & Wood in 1868. One of Bristol's best purpose-designed HQ buildings and wantonly destroyed 1964, some years after the compiler had experienced misgivings at the prospect of life as a commercial artist therein. See [2/59] for five chimney stacks.

(91 & 92)   12.10pm 14 April 1964: Redcliff Hill A fine row of C18/19 historic buildings (which included the C17 shot tower off right) above a raised pavement. The railway tunnel under accounted for the single-storey shops. Note the Chemist's pestle and mortar.

Second row: (93)   1.00pm 27 April 1964: Temple Gate C18 & C19 row truncated left and right by demolition. Bristol & West of Eng. Bank *c.*1890 an extreme bravado, John Hare & Co., floorcloths HQ right.

(94)   3.50pm 7 March 1964: Castle Street last shop The new mood, and new scale, creeps up behind the unfashionable.

(95)   12.10pm 31 August 1964: Bedminster Parade, Wixons Kink The denouement [33,34], the road kinked and Wixons still open for business.

(96)   11.25pm 30 August 1964: North St, Stokes Croft Of this C18 block only Cherry Lane (side of Kings) survives.

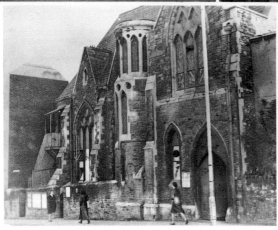

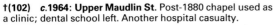

†**(102)   *c.*1964: Upper Maudlin St.** Post-1880 chapel used as a clinic; dental school left. Another hospital casualty.

(103 & 104)   9.30am 24 April 1964: Queen's Road. The popular Carter, Stoffell & Fortt, grocers now no more. Note the salvage sacks on the pavement.

Third row: (97) 12.35pm 30 August 1964: Old Market/Lawford St When a little Georgian house clung to the back of its Old Market neighbour. Now refurbished with consent beyond all good manners.

(98) 4.50pm 25 August 1964: Queen St to Tower Hill Castle moat before covering in and Old Market St uncut by Temple Way.

(99) 10.35am 31 August 1964: Old Market/ Carey's Lane crossing.

†(100) 1964: Park Street in summer with cast-iron lamp standards and the shops beflagged.

†(101) 1964: Broad Weir with the Kingsdown escarpment uninterrupted. The original Broadmead frontages had a distinction (Whiting's) easily lost in refurbishment.

(105) 11.15am 8 March 1964: St James' Parade. C18 & C19 row demolished for Laing Development Co.'s Avon House development.

(106) 3.25pm 27 October 1964: Church St, Temple A setted street behind Yeo Bros [87] lost in redevelopment.

(107)   4.10pm 7 March 1964: Hillgrove St from Dove St This C18 'view-commanding terrace' swept elegantly up the hillside, but compulsory purchase and high rise council flats held greater attraction for those in power with no eyes to see nor ears to hear.

†(108)   *c*.1963: Gay Street This steeper street resorted to stepped pavements, with doorways off the landings. [**18/133**].

†(109)   *c*.1963: Spring Hill from King Square The threat to Georgian Kingsdown had started a decade earlier. By 1963 the battle for the lower slope had been lost to the City Engineer, Architect, Public Health Dept & Housing Committee. This axial roadway is presently under threat again from a greedy housing association scheme. The fanlight right removed in 1986 without consent.

†(110)   *c*.1964: Blenheim Square This will suffice to illustrate Betjeman's 'residential quiet' of a late Georgian pedestrian layout.

†(111 & 112) *c.*1964: **Dove St** Late Georgian artisan houses at the foot of the gardens of C18 1st grade houses, mostly demolished.

†(113) *c.*1964: **Horfield Rd,** corner Southwell St. Georgian group left mostly dem. *c.*1974, C19 row right dem. *c.*1970

†(114) *c.*1964: **Horfield Road** A late Georgian terrace with Tuscan Doric porches demolished for road widening and hospital employees' cars. Provided valuable linkage with the city, foretelling Kingsdown by *gravitas.*

†(115) *c.*1964: **Spring Hill** The inimitable bow and canted bay prior to demolition. The steps and pavement surfaces are now in urgent need of repair.

†(116) *c.*1964: **Rear of C18 houses in Duke St** from gardens in Dove St. The CPAB had included these houses in its list of properties to be retained at all costs put to the public inquiry.

†(117) *c.*1964: **Montague Place,** corner of Alfred Pl. Georgian artisan houses adjacent Kingsdown Brewery (later shoe factory), dem.

†(118) *c.*1964: **Paul St from Oxford St** The authorities treated this second Kingsdown area similarly, its architectural quality making defence harder. Under mounting pressure redeveloped with a scheme of merit.

†(119) *c.*1964: **Nos 10–16 Paul St** Also dem. for High Kingsdown.

†(121) *c.*1964: **Marlborough Hill** Two late Georgian houses, one with canted gable end, dem. for hospital staff car parking under Crown immunity.

†(120) **Early 1960's: Alfred Place** Listed late Georgian houses now all cemented over, mostly without consent. In 1975 an alternative house was constructed on the waste site distant and occupied until action by the authorities. The last two listed houses dem. in redevelopment pleading safety with no attempt to keep a surviving iron lamp-holder.

†(122) *c.*1964: **Kington Buildings** off Portland St. A Georgian passage of 8 houses dem. for the sports centre.

†(123) *c.*1964: **Alfred Pl** from Paul St. A *c.*1870's terrace with living over the shop surviving although as yet unlisted.

†(124) *c.*1964: **Gay St** The last late Georgian house props air.

*(125 & 126) July 1972: **Kingsdown Street Fair,** an annual celebration of conservation area status. A local architect as auctioneer.

(127)   11.20am 30 August 1964: **Stokes Croft** Parking restriction signs could be varied by use of the half circle. The public passageway behind removed in redevelopment of the listed building right.

†(128) **Nos 8 & 9 Albemarle Row, Clifton** Spa lodging houses of 1760's with last surviving original yellow roughcast overlaid with C19 Bristol Black plaster. Granby House yet to be badly flatted.

†(129) *c.*1964: **Nos 302–308 Hotwell Road** C18 wrought-iron gates with swept apex intact at 302 & 304.

†(130)   *c.*1964: **Glendale, behind Granby Hill, Clifton,** a declivity politely declining.

(131)   5.10pm 7 March 1964: **25 Grove Road, Redland** Gentle Gothick to close a garden view, apparently treated as in [**128**], dem.

†(132)   *c.*1964: **Hotwell Road** The raised pavement ends at the General Draper PH on Hinton Lane, dem.

(133 & 134)   31 August & 4 September 1964: **Cumberland Basin bridges** The box girder bridge dwarfing Brunel's 1848 tubular swing bridge distant left and Howard's 1870 copy foreground.

†(135)   5 November 1964: **Netham** bridges over the lock to the Feeder, replaced with Bailey types.

(136 & 137) 3.45pm 26 October 1963 & 9.35am 24 January 1964: **The Embassy cinema, Queens Ave** Bristol's only building with futurist pretensions? Interior during dem.

(138) 11.45pm 28 August 1964: **Upper Berkeley Place** Despite efforts to save Rock Court, off left middle distance, convenient storm damage, the promise of Clifton Heights (as it was then seen) and road plans sufficed to remove this streetscape.

(139) 3.40pm 25 August 1964: **All Saints, Pembroke Rd** G E Street's 1864–8 narrow-aisled master-piece after bombing & post-war dem. See [18/145] for extent of war damage.

Below:
(140) 12.20pm 30 August 1964: **Hippodrome, St Augustine's Pde** after dem. of F Matcham's globe, roof, and attic storey.

(141) 3.10pm 5 October 1964: **Broad Quay** The site of Bristol & West building, completed '67. Dem. of the Garricks Head etc. in '80 for an extension was part of pre-'64 agreement to permit the tower in order to secure road widening at all costs, of course destroying the variety of townscape in the process. Marsh St ruined by Viewlet Ltd & Prop. Hold. & Invest. Trust's speculative offices.

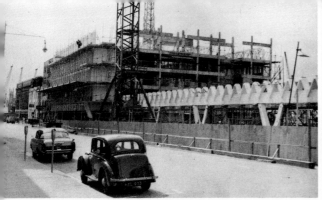

†(142) *c.*1964: **Prince St, The Unicorn Hotel & Car Park** A box-like hotel but car park of verve and ingenuity, marred by the loss of its predecessors.

(143) **11.05am 8 March 1964: Frogmore St** The Entertainment Centre supplants Elizabethan on Stoney Hill. The Georgian home of the University awaits their dem. right. Left the new Folk House [242].

(144) **10.00am 28 August 1964: Colston Street, Radiant House** Fine HQ of Bristol Gas Co. in Portland Stone, 1935 by Whinney, Son and Austen Hall. Self-assured, provincial Modern, which makes a successful turn into Pipe Lane and the surviving side façade of 1904 Gas HQ by W Venn Gough.

(145) **12.05pm August 1964: Site of St John's Arch** Peep-watching Pithay House rise from basement of Fry's No. 7 factory [77] with remains of city wall in angle of basement, centre. Everard's printing works and Georgian John Street to be redevelopment. The distinguished labour exchange potentially at risk.

†(146) *c.*1964: **Corn St, Lloyds Bank lantern 1854, restored** Chosen by John Totterdill as his bank on account of the building.

(147)   2.10pm 18 October 1968:
The Cathedral The C15 St George
& Dragon candelabra from Temple
Church then hung in the
Elder Lady Chapel.

†**(148)   *c*.1964:**
St Stephen's Church Tower Ralph
Edwards doing what all church
architects have to do, deal with
flagpole mountings! He restored the
pierced pinnacles, reminiscent of
masts in this sailors church.

(149)   3.30pm 6 June 1964:
The Cathedral F C Jones
awarding Patricia Harvey, first
winner of John Latimer prize
for historical essays.

(150)   12.20pm 10 March 1964:
Cumberland Road Fine Gothick
with its original garden now
lowered and gated piers removed.

*****(151)   April 1964: Kings
Weston House** Pete West
steadies the compiler's sculpture
whilst at the School of
Architecture.

(152)   2.30pm 7 March 1964:
Redland Hill House, the entrance to
an C18 semi-detached [18].

†**(153)   *c*.1964: Whitby Road**
Brunel's Tudor-arched railway bridge
across the Avon, masked from view
each side and notably missing from the
statutory list.

**(154) 4.05pm
12 May 1964: Bedminster,** between Essex St & Catherine Mead St. The line of Dean Lane Pit railway.

**(155) 11.50am
18 September 1964:
Ashton Gate** The sign on the distant grass reads 'Ashton Gate Platform'. Rownham House distant left.

**(156) 12.00 noon
18 September 1964:
Rownham Hill** Rownham House, dower house to Ashton Court, under demolition for town houses. The Victorians appear to have added a monumental saloon over the wing of the earlier house, itself an apparently altered house of early in the century. Were the battlements commandeered from the existing building, or indeed from Ashton Court?

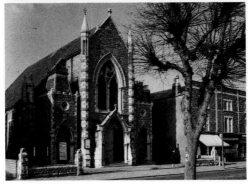

**(157) 3.50pm
8 March 1964: 707
Fishponds Rd** Methodist church of 1894.

**(158) 11.05am
30 August 1964: Ashley
Down Rd** Provincial Gothic Revival house of 1860's.

(159)　11.45am 8 April 1964: Alpenfels, Leigh Woods A large 1890's house of rather stark design, given a very elaborate dressing of carved wook and deep overhanging eaves to create a Swiss 'chalet', perhaps echoing the early C18 enchantment of Leigh Woods on one side and a former counterpart thought to have stood on Observatory Hill opposite. Seen prior to sale for conversion to flats.

(160)　11.30am 31 August 1964: Oakenhill Farm, Brislington C17/C18 farmhouse extant, before cementing.

(161)　12.15pm 8 March 1964: The Shrubberies, Brislington between the former White Hart Hill and the church. A C17 farmhouse of the South Gloucestershire type with cheese loft and rear stair projection, gazebo left facing the church. Probably gentrified pre-1826. Presumably dem. in redevelopment for shops.

19█5

Evening Post, Monday, October 18

Historic buildings

It is splendid news that the condition of some of the houses in Orchard Street will be improved by the combined efforts of the owners, the Ministry of Public Buildings and Works and Bristol Corporation.

This happy co-operation augurs well for the future of those gems of architecture that we have left to us.

At the same time, concern may be expressed at the future of Temple Parish. One hears that the present replanning envisages the complete demolition of the present scene with the exception of Temple Church and the Shakespeare Inn.

What then is the future of Dr White's Almshouses and the delightful corner of Temple rectory? It is important that the latter should be preserved. It is such a part of the church precinct that it seems a great pity if this 17th-century building has to go.

May we have an official statement, please?

REECE WINSTONE

Official Corporation spokesman states: The Planning Department are investigating the possibility of retaining the whole or part of the Temple rectory building. The site of Dr White's Almshouse is required for the new central fire station and it has not been possible to retain this long slim building, which runs right through the middle of the site in the revised layout. An alternative site for the almshouse will be provided in the Redcliffe area where they are to be set in a much more pleasant environment.

(162 & 163)
17 July 1965:
Temple Rectory
Despite the stabilization of the shell of Temple Church this charming frontispiece and the footway to the north were dem.

(164)   10.25am
17 July 1965:
Temple Rectory
Apparently a pair of C17 timber-framed houses needlessly dem. for Norfolk House office development by Temple Church Ecclesiastical Trustees against the efforts of preservationists. Note the pennant paving.

†**(165)   *c*.1964:**
Dr White's
Almshouses, Temple
St The Gothick range by Edward Brigden [**5/68**], 1823, to the C17 rows of almshouses behind [**32/273**]. Plate [**97**] gives the lie to the necessity of demolishing this range for the back yard of the new fire station.

(166)   11.40am
15 January 1965:
Redcliff St
Robinson's flag lowered on the death of Sir Winston Churchill.

(167)   10.00am 17 August 1966: **Cumberland Basin, montage,** opened April 1965. Brunel's tubular bridge spans the lock. The apotheosis of the City Engineer's road schemes; others to be curtailed by growing opposition.

†(168)   *c.*1965: **Hotwell Rd** Traffic backs up due to docking at North Entrance lock by SS *Harry Brown, Steep Holm* & *Stamford.*

(169)   3.30pm 6 March 1965: **Hotwell Rd** Training ship HMS *Flying Fox* at Gas Ferry steps, built 1916 as a class 24 sloop, reconstructed 1923 as an HQ ship, scrapped Aug. 1972.

(170)   *c.*1965: **Prince St Bridge** *Monica Bratt* from Göteborg passes the swing bridge & hydraulic accumulator tower, S&P electric travelling crane left.

†(171)   5 November 1965: **Marsh Bridge, Avon St** Bridge services grubbed out prior to rebuilding.

†(172)   7 March 1964: **Y & Z Sheds, Canon's Marsh** by Mouchel-Hennebique 1906, 1st transit sheds & 1st with 30 cwt rooftop travelling cranes, dem. 1990 by City Council [**364**].

(173)   8.00pm 7 July 1965: **The Grove** *Shetland Trader*, Lerwick, under S&P electric travelling cranes 16, 17 & 18.

(174)   10.20am 17 July 1965: Castle Moat piling for Tower Hill ambulance station, opened October 1966. Is this where the image on the City arms arose? Would we succeed in stopping it being treated thus today?

(175)   11.05am 14 November 1965: Union St, Broadmead Baptist Chapel c.1860, redeveloped as first-floor chapel. Lewis's roof garden still with its glazed ambulatory.

(176 & 177)   January 1967 & August 1965: Trenchard St & Lodge St   The Countess of Huntingdon's Connection gives a verticality to steep Georgian Lodge St. Chapel & left side dem. for a grassed strip and untidy car parking spaces.

**(178) 10.30am 1 January 1965:
17–19 Upper Maudlin St** A court
of six houses *c.*1840 with
contemporary shops and shop
fronts dem. for the BRI.

**(179) 10.35am 15 January 1965:
Brunswick Sq** by Geo. Tully
and its approach through his
Cumberland St (1766) seen here
more or less intact. The west side
was never completed beyond
No. 16. First limes, now flowering
cherries replace the elms! Note
the C19 wrought-iron seat.

**(180) 8.15pm 7 July 1965:
Brunswick Sq** A Paty-like south
side; note the window and
pilaster rhythm. Perhaps the first
facading consent granted by the
planning authority having been
directed otherwise at public
inquiry, becoming in the process
a 'double-pile' development of
Bond St House – a lucrative and
entirely destructive scheme. The
side entrances became dummies
with 14"-high steps! Gloucester
St, left, suffered the first examples
of restoration by virtue of inserted
steel frames upon which were set,
inter alia, chimney stacks! Note
the surviving tops of Gothick
sashes in the Venetian window.

Right *(181) *c.*1965:
Lower Ashley Rd Bridge over the
Froom. The two left-hand houses,
unlisted, survive the M32 exit
demolitions, and are currently
having to be defended. Centre a
flood marker now lost. The 1889
floods in this road were not quite
high enough to allow the boats
carrying bread to clear the tops of
house railings [**6/page 345**],
[**12/33**].

**(182) 12.30pm 2 November
1965: The 1882 flood marker in
Mina Rd.** Was the water level the
centre of circle or top of casting?

(183) 11.30am 19 January 1965: Hope Square, Clifton The two built sides of a trapezoidal square completed only by the flanks of Albemarle Row & Hope Chapel. Note Thos. Paty's original arrangement, brick over plastered basements, but the falls resulted in uneven entrances in and below the 3 principal storeys. Shortly to be dem.

†**(184)** *c.*1965: **Tucked in the angle of Hope Sq.** an arched passage to Glendale & Clifton

(185) 2.25pm 28 October 1965: The Promenade The limes dwarf Camp House, Chas. Dyer 1831, felled in *c.*1976.

(186) 11.45am 2 November 1965: Pembroke Road It seems unlikely to have been old enough to be the hanging tree, as suggested when was felled

†**(187) 31 July 1965: The Observatory, Clifton** Camera Obscura installed 1829 probably in a former windmill. Ghyston's Cave was opened in 1837

Left (188) 4.05pm 20 August 1965: Pennywell Rd/Plummer St (right). Scattered C18 development backing on to the Froom, left, rebuilt C19 for commercial uses. In C20 timber merchants and companies based here.

Above †(189) 19 September 1965: Easton, looking east to the high-rise housing on the Outer Circuit Road.

*(190 & 191) March 1965: Arno's Castle, Junction Rd 1764, probably by James Bridges in black slag. Stables, coach-house, brewery & laundry to Arno's Court, formerly in greensward, now concrete and awkwardly painted. Two towers were thus treated, removing a gorgeous 14" brick boundary wall.

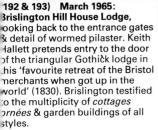

192 & 193) March 1965: Brislington Hill House Lodge, looking back to the entrance gates & detail of wormed pilaster. Keith Hallett pretends entry to the door of the triangular Gothick lodge in his 'favourite retreat of the Bristol merchants when got up in the world' (1830). Brislington testified to the multiplicity of *cottages ornées* & garden buildings of all styles.

194) 12.05pm 2 November 1965: St John's Church, Bedminster filling its yard. John Norton's church of 1855 after blitz' damage, awaiting clearance [226].

1966

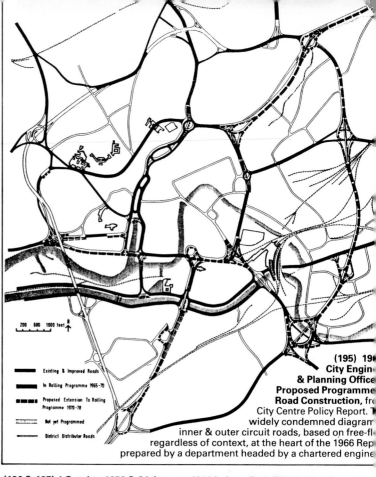

The new road system

The map in the R.I.B.A. Journal with Mrs Rowntree's article on Bristol, shows the City Engineer's plans for the new road system.

Excellent as it is to restore Queen Square to its former quiet, by taking the arterial road through Prince Street and along The Grove, it is a matter of concern as to the line over the Froom to Canon's Marsh.

From the map, the future road seems to go straight off The Grove to Canon's Marsh through that complex of 18th/19th century buildings, the Shakespeare Hotel and the Bush warehouse.

Can we afford the loss of these outstandingly fine examples of architecture? Or is there room for the new (one way) road around the end of the Bush building on the water's edge?

REECE WINSTONE

▬▬▬	Existing & Improved Roads
▬▬	In Rolling Programme 1965-70
▬ ▬ ▬	Proposed Extension To Rolling Programme 1970-78
·····	Not yet Programmed
———	District Distributor Roads

200   600   1000 feet

(195) 196 City Engine & Planning Office Proposed Programme Road Construction, fro City Centre Policy Report. T widely condemned diagram inner & outer circuit roads, based on free-flo regardless of context, at the heart of the 1966 Rep prepared by a department headed by a chartered engine

(196 & 197) 4 October 1959 & 24 January 1940 below: Redcliff Hill Shot Tower William Watts' dreamt-invention of patent shot of 1782 preserved this C17 house until condemned by the above road plan. Failure to execute the proposed road junction meant its dem. was entirely unnecessary. 185 years of process at the top of the tower. **[18/191]**.

Save shot tower

It seems that the plan proposed by the former City Architect, Mr Nelson Meredith, has not found favour with the designers of the widened Redcliff Hill at this point, namely for the unique shot tower to be left on an island site and reached by a subway....

Remember, Watt's Shot Tower was the first one – others followed in London, Chester and Newcastle, which have, I believe, all gone.

We ought to save it. Is there no crusading voice in the City Council for the preservation of such a unique historic building?

REECE WINSTONE

(198)   10.10am 15 October 1966: North St, Stokes Croft
The road to Gloucester past the C17 Full Moon PH, bereft of its
pretty hanging moon below the iron overthrow. C18 & 19
buildings left, dem.

†(199)   30 July 1966: 53 West St, St Philip's
From funeral directors and hairdressers to a
betting office. For details of preceding owners
prior to this decline see [**37/154**].

(200)   12.15pm 9 May 1966: Temple Colston's School, Victoria St Foster & Wood, 1862, the French-style winner of a
competition, seen here after loss of tower roof and cupola on the 1870's (?) master's house oriel. If of two dates still not
entirely married to the 1870's commercial rows seen in [**82, 83**].

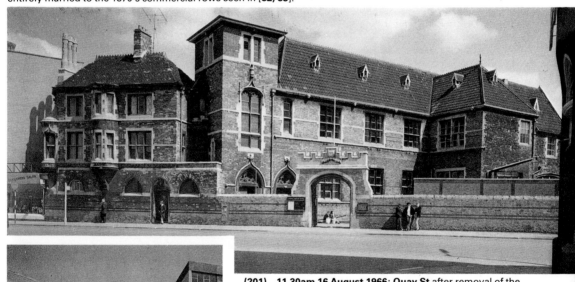

(201)   11.30am 16 August 1966: Quay St after removal of the
St Lawrence balancer to St John's nave by crass St Lawrence
'House' office block.

**(202)   4.45pm 16 August 1966: Prewett St glass
cone** of c.1780's from the south entrance-way after
reduction to present height in 1930's. Asbestos roof
replaced with asbestos slates in conversion and all
outbuildings dem.

(203 & 204) 16 August & 15 October 1966: Brandon Steep & Cumberland St Gothick detailing was often coupled with Palladian windows and laced glazing bars in C18 Bristol, and was often charmingly unconvincing (full-blooded in [48, 190]. The Cumberland St premises well cared-for (misused the other side), compares with Fuller-Eberle's gift to Savages of Brandon Cottage, left without laced glazing by Bristol Building Preservation Trust in 1988 refurb.

(205)   10.10am 15 October 1966: Upper York St West side, C18 house dem. for ESA Robinson (Holdings) spec. office block, Brunswick House.

(206)   10.30am 15 October 1966: Ellbroad St seen from Carey's Lane (now Temple Way) looking west to Lower Castle St. The last, C18, house dem. December.

(207)   10.55am 9 May 1966: Rock Court, Berkeley Pl. A stepped and ramped pavement & roadway to C18 artisan houses dem. for a multi-storey car park.

(208)   10.05am 3 March 1966: Berkeley Pl. with Rock Ct entry C18 row with Maggs' 3-bay 1930's cabinet & bedding works, right.

(209) 9.15am 4 April 1966: Grand Spa Ballroom, Clifton Art Deco lighting in Philip Munro's once splendid 1893 interior.

(210) 10.10am 3 March 1966: Regent St, Clifton Post Office The late lamented PO & lantern.

(211) 4.30pm 17 August 1966: Students' Union, Queen's Rd opened Sept. 1965 with the longest bar in the west(?). Loss of fine screen of trees on both sides renders group out of scale with the neo-classical terrace facing.

(212) 5.00pm 16 August 1966: Dept of Chemistry, University Walk A mosaic *tableau* curiously sited over lecture rooms and foyers fails to make a sense of place from a terrace with spectacular vista.

(213) 9.35am 4 March 1966: Jacob's Wells Rd Cat, dog and horse are illustrated on the enamelled RSPCA advertisement, sited on a hill much used by horse-drawn vehicles.

*(214) **March 1966: V & W Sheds, Canon's Road** from Unicorn car park, with cranage intact. Royal Hotel block in Trinity St, red brick tobacco bond, centre, and Rowe Bros warehouse dem. for Royal Hotel redevelopment 1989.

Below (217) 3.50pm 5 March 1966: Barton Hill, Gt Western Cotton Factory 1838, cast-iron columns internally, spinning block dem. 1968 after use from 1925 as rayon mill and warehouse. Weaving shed dem. later. Note castellated tank room and line of former quay for loading. Engine house left? A venture undercut by cheap rail charges from Liverpool.

Above, right (218) 5.45pm 16 August 1966: Cumberland Basin When fountains could camouflage traffic pollution.

(221) **5.20pm 15 August 1966: Redcliff Bridge** c.1942, bascule control room recently intact, from Redcliff Pde frames a milling panorama. WV Gough's WCA feed mill, 1898, right dem. and WCA warehouse beyond listed & 'at risk' since 1980. Welsh Back granary, left, & Proctor Baker's right distant, spoilt in re-use with grant aid.

(215) 24 April 1966: Narrow Quay with CWS HQ & warehouse of 1905 & V Shed, left. A glazed light well on the line of Aldersky Lane generated the plan form of Harris's red & cream brick & faience CWS building. The tower of St Stephen's prominent and note the barges moored at Narrow Quay.

(216) 6.00pm 16 August 1966: Hotwell Rd New memorial to Samuel Plimsoll, inventor of the safe loading line for ships.

Above, left †(219) 30 July 1966: Bathurst Wharf Stothert & Pitt electric travelling cranes 21 & 22 on 1867 wharf (listed shed, 1875, behind dem.). *Swinford* steel barge foreground.

Above †(220) June 1966: Narrow Quay Steel barges *Weston* & *Excel* with SS *Woodwren*, London, at W Shed. Nos 20 & 22 Narrow Quay adjacent Bush warehouse.

†(222) 31 July 1966: Wapping Wharf Built 1874–6 as terminus of Harbour Railway. S&P 5-ton cranes, Nos 33–36, set up in 1965 in short-lived attempt to revive handling facilities. MH *Kenn* services the grab.

(223 & 224) 12.20pm 9 May 1966: Mill Lane, Bedminster East St to Paul St, about where Dalby Ave now intersects, a domed cast-iron urinal with guarded & serpentine pathway. Dem. on grounds that it was not of Bristol manufacture! And the gents' view looking up.

(225)   12.40pm 4 February 1966: 46 High St, Westbury-on-Trym Wm Townsend, chemists, Edwardian fittings in contemporary shop. 'Genuine Horse & Cattle Medicines'.

(226)   11.50am 30 November 1966: St John's Church, Bedminster by John Norton, 1855, in dem. after gutting during the blitz' [**32/267**].

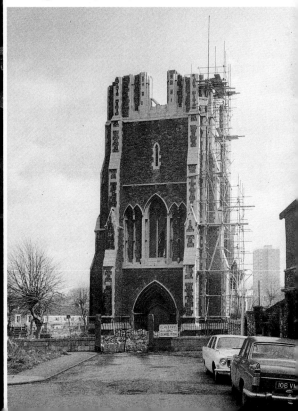

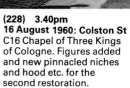

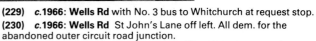

(228) 3.40pm 16 August 1960: Colston St C16 Chapel of Three Kings of Cologne. Figures added and new pinnacled niches and hood etc. for the second restoration.

227) 9.00am 17 August 1966: St Michael's Hill howing Nos 55 & 57 early C19, dem. by the University nd the site left empty. Nos 31-37 await reconstruction.

(229) *c.*1966: **Wells Rd** with No. 3 bus to Whitchurch at request stop.
(230) *c.*1966: **Wells Rd** St John's Lane off left. All dem. for the abandoned outer circuit road junction.

231) 11.20am 18 October 1966: Dean Lane, Bedminster looking orth; Dame Emily (Smythe) Playground (railings that didn't go in var) off left. Clarence Hotel closed 3 October.

(232) 12.15am 30 November 1966: Compton Lodge, 98 Hampton Rd Uncharacteristically plain home of arct. Wm Venn Gough (d.1918) in local sandstone with Bathstone dressings dem. for housing association flats.

1967

Evening Post, Wednesday, May 31

Save this building

That anyone should even contemplate demolishing one of the most original buildings in Bristol – the Everard building in Broad Street – is ridiculous. Whoever is at the back of this proposal for Broad Street shows an absence of appreciation of unique architecture that is unbelievable.

I believe the protests against this plan will astonish even our often hard-pressed planning committee of the City Council.

Let me quote from an interesting and rare book which I possess, published by Edward Everard in 1902, shortly after its erection:

"As a printer, the loyalty and fealty due to the memory of my progenitors in the art, took overwhelming possession of the mind. I have the fullest appreciation for what is beautiful in architecture, but paramount is the reverence and regard inspired by men like Gutenberg, Fust, Schoeffer, Coster and Caxton, who have made the printing press the vehicle of the world's mind.

". . . I fearlessly assert notwithstanding the many preconceived impressions during the several stages of construction, that thousands have since visited here many times to acquaint themselves of the illuminated allegories in the Doulton ceramic art.

"In placing this illuminated front in the city of my adoption, the all-powerful force of raising things anew out of the ashes of the past was my inspiring motive. I am a printer heart and head and hand, and to have the privilege of glorifying men like those before-mentioned, whose pulses beat today in every revolution of the world's press, is a joy for which I do not account myself worthy."

The original Everard works extending from John Street into Little John Street are again worthy of preservation, at least externally.

To combat demolition of good architecture in the heart of the city, I understand the council has declared the part within the circle of the original town wall to be designated a "special area". This, I suggest, is a very special case in a very special area. May the callous, tasteless blunder of putting a sky-scraper next door to St John's Church never be repeated.

REECE WINSTONE

(233 & 234)   10.00am 22 July 1967: Tucker Street left, Bath Street right Part of Paty's 1792 Bristol Bridge approaches development which formed a wide thoroughfare to Counterslip, leaving the line of medieval Tucker St to be formed by a neat triangular block with flat-iron ends. Secondhand bookseller R J Beard apparently retains his original Georgian bowed shopfront (no sign board rises up to the window sill band). The directories indicate the shop had been booksellers since 1850 , and in the 1880's James George (later of Christmas Steps?). Paty's block was similarly arranged at the Counterslip end. Demolished for ease of the brewers' lorries, just as part of Bath St was to be in 1986. Today most of Bath St has been railed off as private property, but no explanation of this was given at the public inquiry.

(235)   2.20pm 9 June 1990: Broad Street Henry Williams for Everard's Press, 1900. Arts & Crafts façade based on three arches of St John's arch. Tiles designed by W J Neatby for Doulton & Co. in conjunction with Williams & Everard, tiled by Walter Yoxall. The terracotta printing works façade stretching along much of John St was brought down by Legal & General's nasty 1972 redevelopment which flooded the right edge of the Broad St facade.

(236)   12.15pm 9 July 1967: Sts Philip & Jacob church, Tower Hill E W Godwin's fine, canopied monument to Rev Wm (illegible), vicar, in the south aisle, destroyed to no purpose other than fashion, presumably with Faculty.

(237) 11.15am 29 May 1967: St George's Rd, Fuller's Carriage Works, later Central Institute, Ed. Gabriel 1891. Right-hand bays later. Got down 20 years ago in order to create a development site. Nos 19 & 21 right C18, listed, façades dem. & reconstructed 1990 without consent.

(238) 12.05pm 9 July 1967: Colston Ave The well-trod side alley to the C18 Artichoke upper bar, refuge of actors and Little Theatre-goers, right. The 1870's polychrome block, similar to 2 & 4 Victoria St, balancer to the Co-op HQ , dem. for River Rd Prop. Invest. Co. development. The PH was 'Under the Bank' and had fronted the Float.

(239) 11.50am 9 July 1967: Rupert St/Bridewell St A consistent 2-colour brick group of 1900 and 1890 at the Crown & Dove PH.

(240) 5.30pm 15 June 1967: Rupert St panorama CWS Bristol Depot, right, leased 1888 extended into centre section in 1890's, prior to acquisition of Broad Quay site, later occupied by Lindrea and Inkerman respectively. Now site of Law Courts.

(241) 10.45am 29 May 1967: Park Row Vandyke Press by Mowbray Green, 1913, now University Dept of Drama and recently suffering damage from cement ribbon pointing. Unlisted but 'notably in touch with the modern movement' (Gomme).

(242) 10.30am 29 May 1967: Stoney Hill site of Prince's Theatre. Georgian home of University below University tower with Forum Gallery flat-roofed addition below again – makes for a depressing scene.

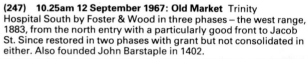

(246)   10.15am 12 September 1967: Old Market
Trinity Hospital North with founder's Edwardian (?)
statue, last rebuilt dully by Frank Wills in 1913, founded
1395 by John Barstaple.

(247)   10.25am 12 September 1967: Old Market Trinity
Hospital South by Foster & Wood in three phases – the west range,
1883, from the north entry with a particularly good front to Jacob
St. Since restored in two phases with grant but not consolidated in
either. Also founded John Barstaple in 1402.

†(243)   20 March 1967: **Broadmead** C A Walker's 1932 equestrian bronze of John Wesley before his stable behind the Grade I entrance screen wall to the New Room, partly rebuilt in pennant in 1954.

†(244)   21 January 1967: **Peter St** St Peter's Church and the car parks that made use of the basements of the blitz' shops for so many years. St Peter's had probably lost its plaster before the C19 making it look, like all medieval buildings of rubblestone, coarse and rustic. It also accelerates decay; will it be replastered in the completion of Castle Park?

(245)   12.20pm 9 July 1967: **Castle St from Tower St** An intact horizon left of St Peter's, marred to the right. The streets here newly municipalised.

(248)   11.15am 14 July 1967: **Old Market** C17, derelict by 1974 and largely dem. in restoration. 3-D blocked and blended sign 'John Goss' at 38 & 39. Thought good enough to feature in a book on shops in 1981 but nevertheless a pastiche shop front and windows substituted. Typical of RW's best work; the shot always includes the context.

(249, 250, 251, 252)   5 January, 8 July, 9 June, 22 July 1967: **Roads in the making:** site of outer circuit road at Co-operative Buildings, Barton Hill; Temple Way underpass and Temple Gate 'temporary' flyover (still extant today). Note the Police call box and the CRS electric milk float.

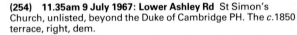

Below (253)   12.15pm 31 May 1967: Philip St, Bedminster The last occupants at No. 89. 1870's with a late Georgian house in centre shot. Note the gas lantern.

(254)   11.35am 9 July 1967: Lower Ashley Rd St Simon's Church, unlisted, beyond the Duke of Cambridge PH. The c.1850 terrace, right, dem.

(257)   11.00am 5 January 1967: Bottom row – Four designs for turning narrow corners: Leadhouse Rd & Co-operative Buildings, Barton Hill Note the local cigarette advertising hung over from Christmas.

(258)   5.10pm 17 June 1967: Easton Rd, Clarence Rd, Lawrence Hill A commercial block c.1900 of impressive size with earlier manufactories at left, decrepit in part 1990. Left and right sides all dem. by 1990.

†(255) *c.*1967: **Wells Rd, Totterdown** The three lamps junction with the fine *c.*1840 pair commencing the scene pre the Exeter line. All taken for outer circuit road interchange.

†(256) *c.*1967: **Wells Rd, Totterdown** Bush Hotel right, unlikely materials for a bank, centre, favoured by C F W Dening. YMCA survived the clearances.

(259) 11.40am 1967: **Millpond St/Lower Ashley Rd** Brickwork painted over centre, mid C19 at the White Lion PH, right, an area totally blighted by M32.

†(260) 12 November 1967: **Regent St (left), St Philip's** Painted brickwork again of *c.*1840. Shutters up for the last time at No. 76.

†(261) 25 February 1967: Canon's Rd Wharf 1965 Cranage on Wapping Wharf, 30-cwt electric Stothert & Pitt cranes top the historic industrial aesthetic of Y & Z Sheds, fixed derrick and crane No. 7. The 20-ton coaling crane off right. All add up to a powerful landscape, now entirely removed, mostly since conservation area designation despite objections, and the quay wall reduced to boot.

†(262) 5 July 1967: Gas Ferry Road, Albion Dockyard Chas. Hill's grab dredger *Clifton* for PBA launched by Mrs F Martin. Hill's closed 1977 whereafter what remained of the working port soon disappeared. The slips were converted for leisure craft use.

†(263) September 1967: Avonmouth Docks The infamous call stand system of engaging dockers on a daily basis ended 18 September with the introduction of decasualisation.

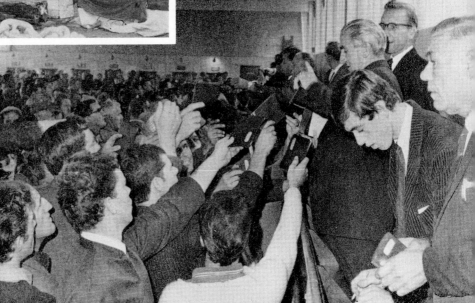

†(264) 11 February 1967: The Grove, West Mud Dock
Site of Padmore's Georgian crane, by this time travelling crane 9 had become encased in concrete and was under an awning, perhaps to protect the newspaper bales seen carried by *Rhodesia*. C19 handcrane left; Bush warehouse (formerly Acraman's) with its railings and its glazing bars just visible on the original, but without its new, oversize attic storey.

(265) 11.35am 29 June 1967: Canon's Rd
Bristol & Clifton Oil Gas Works at Sea Banks first established 1823, manufacturing coal gas from 1836 and amalgamated 1853 as Bristol United Gas Light Co. Wooden setted coaling jetty in front of the office block possibly by W. Fiddies *c*.1853 (much reduced) at the centre of a large and severe pennant stone group presently at risk from plans of the three landowners, City Council, British Gas and Rail.

(266) 11.25am 29 June 1967: Canon's Rd, Gas Works Ferry Commenced 1830's for shipwrights working on Brunel's ships, run by Docks Committee from 1903 and closed pre-1967. This is in fact the Sea Cadets. The gas lantern and bracket have gone and consent to dem. McArthur's beyond has been granted, against the advice of CAP.

(267)   10.40am 17 August 1967: Bedford Place, Kingsdown north side, right-hand end of row, with Granville Place behind trees, seen from Bedford Rd. RW's white Anglia 1 PHT where the roadway necks down today. A charming group with right three houses c.1800, those to left c.1820, all compulsorily purchased and dem. for waste ground by Health Authority.

(268)   5.20pm 15 June 1967: Nos 70–78 Stokes Croft 74 & 76 by E W Godwin, unlisted, the shopfront to 74 removed without conservation area consent. No. 78 a C18 5-bay house, later Christian Science Reading Rm dem. with a former Baptist College off left for a spec. office block.

(269)   10.55am 29 May 1967: Lower Church Lane, St Michael's Hill looking east, former rectory distant. Left side dem. for University purposes and left as a car park to date. Offices of Harvey Barton & Son Ltd fine art publishers left and their works in the four-gabled building, post 1883. A picturesque design seen in context by RW.

(270)   11.45am 29 May 1967: Dighton St Harford House, an RC convent from 1846 (chapel left, c.1860), the Harford family's fine 5-bay Palladian townhouse c.1760 with flanking wing to right apparently raised. Overrun with housing co-operative flats in 1970's.

(271) 5.05pm 15 June 1967: Elmgrove Rd, Cotham Grove Baptist Church by Hans Price of Weston-super-Mare 1871, in local pennant and with less virtuoso than when in Weston. Seen in demolition for houses.

(272) 10.30am 17 August 1967: Granville Place, Alfred Hill from Cottage Place. Attic sills dropped, one of a row of four fine Regency houses shortly before dem. by Hospital Board for waste ground. Note the setted Alfred Hill, presently at risk.

(273) 3.00pm 3 January 1967: Trinity St/ Place, Easton Demolition of c.1860 before hard hats and Health & Safety at Work Act.

(274) 3.35pm 6 April 1968: Horfield Rd What it was all about; construction of the new BRI and Radiography Dept.

(275) 10.00am 5 January 1967: Dalby Ave site, Bedminster
Bristol Tannery, dem., when? Malago right.

(276) 12.30pm 79 Coronation Rd
Businessman's villa mid-C19, in salubrious
Coronation Rd, dem. for a filling station.

**(277) 12.30pm 17 November 1967:
52 Cumberland Rd** Even finer, *c*.1820, when
Cumberland Rd was dignified. Dem. for
Hospital Board service vehicle standing!

†(278) 4 February 1967: Albert Rd
scrapyards, Totterdown bridge and engine
shed left. Site of wholesale fruit market.

(279)   11.45am 9 April 1967: Shrubbery Rd, Downend Horse tramcar of Bristol Tramways & Carriage Co. See [**12/75**] for background.

280)   11.50am 4 September 1967: College Rd Early C20 cast-iron lamp standard with city arms and its replacement. Note the salvage sack.

281)   4.15pm 4 March 1967: Radley Rd, Fishponds The former vicarage c.1850, later Parklands High School, dem.

(282)   8.05pm 16 June 1967: Lawrence Hill Pack Horse PH c.1850 & 1880. Presumably this was then under threat, or RW believed so.

1968

Evening Post, Monday, May 27

Build tower block away from centre

Brutal Plan

The most ghastly thing that has happened in post-war Bristol, in my opinion, is the erection of a tower block alongside and completely dwarfing the medieval church. I refer to the horrible mistake in Quay Street where St John's-on-the-Wall is made to look ridiculous.

It is even worse than that other horror, the ugliest chimney in England, spoiling Royal Fort House and the incomparable skyline of our noble city.

Therefore, congratulations to the Evening Post leader writer and for the opinions of distinguished architects of this city. Scrap the Post Office 300 foot monstrosity at once and for all time. The city planners must ban all such towers from the central area to preserve our heritage of a medieval city. Keep them on the line of the Outer Circuit Road, in Easton, St Philip's Marsh, or Totterdown, two miles from the city centre, if commerce requires them.

I hope all those who admire our city will sign a petition against this brutal proposal.

REECE WINSTONE

(284)   11.00am 15 November 1968: Redcliff Hill, Shot Tower Former city architect Meredith's plan to island site the tower failed and dem. proceeded.

(285)   11.15am 28 January 1968: Redcliff Hill, The Ship Inn This intact *c.*1860's PH formed a group with the shot tower, left. Here you could dance to live music.

Top left (286)   11.40am 28 February 1968: Ship Court, Redcliff Hill The back of Ship Inn — nothing here to prevent the moving of the carriageway! The attractions of a large office block on Redcliff Hill and the flyover intersection were too much for the authorities.

283)   1968: Temple Way/Old Market Note site of Bristol ʉnited Press left on site of Beavis mineral water works; Central ʉll, lower left, Sir Thos Lawrence birthplace bottom centre ʉd new shot tower, top right.

(287) 5.50pm 28 July 1968: Greyfriars, Lewin's Mead Not to be confused with a C17 house surviving in part in Blackfriars slightly to north-east. This, probably C17, stair projection facing, bereft of its stacks, dem. following excavation of med. Greyfriars. The St John's high rise, right. A C18 house, left, in Lewin's Mead.

(288) 11.30am 8 March 1968: 27 Lower Ashley Rd Premises of Hugh Baird & Sons, maltsters. Two Vauxhall Victors, Standard, Ford Zodiac, Morris van and Austin Cambridge on a vacant site.

(289) 4.10pm 24 February 1968: Clifton St, Easton The maltings from the opposite direction.

†(290) 9 March 1968: 18–22 Narrow Quay An C18 ensemble of three, possibly sail or rigging lofts and incorporating a way through to the Shakespeare PH. Brought down for redevelopment claiming safety but ambitions for redevelopment overtaken by conservation area status. Conservationists did not want a replica but an exact copy of the distressed façade (lime roughcast, Bristol Black, cement patching and all) has now been approved!

(291) 11.30am 5 July 1968: The Centre Painted metalwork on one of the Arnolfini's temporary city sculpture sites, possessing a good deal more conviction than that erected permanently in 1971 – see [331]. Sculptor's name please?

(292) 10.55am 2 May 1968: Westbury College College House, c.1709 and resashed, built from remains of C15 college, purchased by public subscription and vested in the National Trust in 1907. Seen here in demolition following a fire and excavation of the collegiate foundations. Site redeveloped for flats for the elderly.

1969

Evening Post, Friday, July 25

Park Street

My apologies to the City Engineers Department if I gave the impression that they were responsible for the choice of lamp posts being erected in Park Street. It so often happens that one assumes it is "they" (the local authority) who make the blunders in taste about our city furniture.

But to learn that it is the Park Street traders themselves who have rejected the suggested graceful wall lanterns is almost unbelievable – it is disastrous! Surely by their action they are damaging the most noble street in Bristol, they are spoiling the classic view of Sir George Oatley's University Tower.

I would think it is committing commercial suicide to "uglify" the street and I venture to suggest that an emergency meeting of the traders be held immediately to reverse the decision.

May I make it clear that I am in complete ignorance of the constitution of the Traders' Committee responsible, but if I were a Park Street trader I would expect to offer the use of my wall free for the erection of graceful lanterns, which beautify historic streets in other towns, and give up to, say, £50 for each premises for the privilege. A sum of £5,000 would then be available, if a financial contribution to the city was appropriate. This is really worth spending money on.

Park Street, it seems to me, is in danger of slipping downhill – garish signs mar the Georgian facades (the rebuilding so courageously enforced by the City Architect 15 years ago); the number of empty shops now stands at eight (eight too many) . . . .

REECE WINSTONE

Evening Post, Wednesday, September

Record library

May I offer congratulations to t chairman and members of the Cultu Committee on the decision to establi the record lending library, with t priority to classical music?

It was in 1947 that you published first plea that we follow in the wake those progressive municipalities w had by then already offered such c tural facilities. By dint of remind through your columns at appro mately two-year intervals, as number of other lucky cities, towns a even villages rose, my 22 years lo campaign ends.

REECE WINSTON

(293)   11.15am 11 July 1969: **Freeland Place, Hotwells** Rownham Hotel visible from south following dem. of C16/17 house on th opposite corner [**31/183**]. The hotel dem. for road widening and a successful new termination made to the c.1830 terrace.

(294)   3.55pm 4 September 1969: St Luke's Road, Bedminster National school 1862 by H Crisp, directory entry under Weare St, left, now removed together with some sixty houses. Plates [**32/266,268**] show the schoolrooms in use and before alteration.

†(295)   27 April 1969: Queen's/Clifton Rd The somewhat coarse graffiti outside the 10 o'clock shop read *Take a day off from insanity/cars pubs telly/supermarkets work/offices police rain/sex wars shopping/Break out Join hands.* This was the year of anti-Vietnam war demonstrations and the Sergeant Pepper LP.

†(296)   19 April 1969: Hotwell Rd The same photographer was also struck by this alternative, scarlet ground-floor storey at No. 116; the shopwindow closed by a fantastic landscape with an oculus in the thatched cottage, presumably as the occupier endeavours to resist the intrusion of the street.

(297) 1.00pm 25 April 1969: Manor Farm, Horfield A barn *c.*1800 in lias, dem. for development. Was Manor Fm south of Kellaway Ave?

(298) 11.30am 12 September 1969: Court Farmhouse, Whitchurch Lane A fine C15 house of manorial status seemingly with complete arch-braced roof, seen after a fire that made clearance for housing easier. Substantial farm buildings followed suit. Another case of rubblestone that had lost its plaster.

(299) 9.00am 25 April 1969: 63 Passage Rd, Westbury-on-Trym House of *c.*1800, possibly added to an earlier structure, said to have been used as the first Westbury police station.

(300)   5.45pm 13 July 1969:
Henleaze Rd Royal School of
Industry for the Blind, 1909, Ed
Gabriel's last work. The attic storey
and bell tower are nicely handled.
Dem. for housing.

(301)   5.00pm 24 April 1969:
63 Passage Rd, from Greystoke Rd
Dem. for nasty block of private flats.

(302)   12.00 noon 10 March 1969: St Gabriel's Church, Australia Place, Easton   J C Neale, 1870, with his C of E School beyond right, of the following year. Certainly an architect with few buildings still extant; this one dem. on spurious grounds, despite being listed (see RW's letters on the subject under 1975).

(303)   12.45pm 12 July 1969: St Gabriel's Church   Chancel arch from the south. Neale's gothic has been described as 'primitive' and 'rather grim'. It was also distinctive and colourful. He was killed by a train at 42.

(304 & 305) 21 October 1969: Holy Trinity Church, Trinity Rd
Commissioner's church of 1829–32 by Rickman and Hutchinson looking west (top) and east (right) whilst still in use. The pews and pulpit are later. Note the fine Gothic organ case and former gasoliers. The interior now ruined and much of the exterior in bad repair: an example of poor secular usage.

(306 & 307)   12.50pm 27 July 1969: St Andrew's Church, Montpelier An aisleless church of *c*.1860's whose budget, despite its hammerbeam roof, prevented it rising above the commonplace. Photographed during dem. following redundancy.

(308)   15 December 1969: Colston Hall, Town Meeting Were you there? RW was, at the end of the sixth row in the centre of plate. This meeting should have convinced the City Council once and for all that Bristolians were not having development on sites created by partial infilling of the harbour (maintenance costs of harbour walls had been a burden hitherto with no solution) and the road scheme published in August *Civic News,* for the audience passed their own motion against the proposals. In fact the response was a Town Poll and many more moves before final abandonment of the Bill.

†(309) 11 May 1969: Wapping MV *John King* heads west past the Fairbairn steam crane of 1876, but otherwise very little activity is apparent.

†(310) 15 February 1970: Sand Wharf (Poole's) from Baltic Wharf River Police, formed 1844, in one of their launches from the River Station on The Grove on duty in a foggy millpond. MV *Badminton* above.

(312) 5.05pm 13 July 1969: St Luke's Church, York Road A close up of cross-gabled north aisle. A design by John Norton, 1861, architect of Holy Trinity, Stapleton, St John's Bedminster [13, 266] and others. One who knew his Geometric and Somerset towers, and chose to interpose gables between the lines of the Georgian parapets. Presumably the spire and second stage pinnacles were never completed. Dem. 1970.

1970

Evening Post, Monday, March 2

Have Bristol's City Fathers no imagination?

May I speak up for two projects in the news at the moment?

It is absolutely essential for the architecture and history of our great city that St Peter's church tower be incorporated into the plans of the Museum and Art Gallery, as envisaged by Sir Hugh Casson, and as shown so admirably at the City Planning Exhibition in Quakers Friars.

Also, I cannot wait any longer to see justice done to the last remaining chambers of the castle above ground (in Tower Street).

It will be a great relief to see the work of c.1227 put on show to all citizens in 1970 – 30 years after the blitz!

I view with much horror, the attitude of the members of the City Council who are dragging their feet in giving support to the preservation of the SS *Great Britain*.

I would not have believed it possible that Bristol could officially turn its back on such a worthwhile enterprise – but we have had experience of this crazy attitude before (The Cross, Friese-Greene's birthplace, Arno's Castle Colonnade, etc., etc.).

Do not our City Fathers have any imagination? Cannot they, at least, try to attract tourists to our truly magnificent city by giving Brunel's ship a suitable harbour, the Lord Mayor to inaugurate an appeal fund, and the offer to double the contributions forthcoming.

Handled by a truly publicity-conscious committee, the benefits would be immense in attracting new tourists to Bristol. It could equal or surpass that already achieved by the Zoo.

I like the ideas put forward by Mr Zealey on behalf of the Junior Chamber of Commerce – but why did not these ideas come from our City Fathers?

Surely they should be the leaders of constructive thought in our city – or are we just unlucky in our rulers?

REECE WINSTONE

**(313)   12.30pm 4 July 1970:
Avonmouth Docks** The ship, as she was
referred to locally, had first berthed at
Avonmouth to undertake a further round
of repairs and necessary installations prior
to navigation of the Avon and the Float.
Note the wooden rope enrichment
bordering the stern lantern, probably
surviving from the original decorative
scheme and now removed.

(314)   9.00am 5 July 1970: Portway SS
Great Britain is towed up the Avon. RW
noted in his negative ledger overhearing
"a rich Bedminster accent say: 'Oh, we've
got a view all ways here, look!'" – a
comment he attributed to it being the
lady's first visit to the Somerset bank.

**(315)   12.15pm 31 July 1970: City
Museum, SS *Gt Britain*** Trotman designed
anchor on temporary display.

**(316 & 317)   5 July 1970:
Cumberland Basin** SS *Gt Britain*
squeezes the locks that had had to
be widened for her egress.
Brunel's wider replacement lock
of 54 ft, precipitated by his ship
and progressed after the horse
had bolted, had been sealed
decades earlier.

**(318)   19 July 1970: Great
Western Dry Dock** The moment
of truth as the ship is edged back
into Brunel's dock of 1839.

**(319)   2.30pm 23 June 1971: SS
*Gt Britain*** The lord mayor
presents the City Council's
felicitations to Jack Hayward,
benefactor, who receives them
on behalf of the Gt Britain
Project. Note the diversity of
Hotwell Rd, before being
submerged under a developers'
and planners' brick cloak.

(320)   11.55am 29 August 1970: Christmas St & Host St One of Bristol's fine surviving groups after loss of the east side of Christmas St. Unfortunately this was followed by dem. of the Host St chimney, part of the C1? warehouse and over-restoration of the jettied fish and chip shop No. 17, a C17 refronting and raising of a C14/15 building. RW had to fight for the restoration of the building on the opposite corner and SPAB successfully resisted sale of the C13 Madonna and Child from St Bartholomew's Hospital gateway. Bristol Municipal Charities however failed to have the fine statue conserved.

(321)   31 May 1970: The Downs A good body of students are addressed on Acts Ch.II v.38. Is it churlish to suppose they are breaking the journey between 'dry' Stoke Bishop halls of residence (a restrictive covenant demands) and Blackboy Hill? Who is the speaker?

1971

Evening Post, Friday, April 23

Brunel offices must be saved

Your news (April 7) of the imminent widening of Temple Gate brings nearer the risk of the planners to demolish Brunel's Great Western Railway offices.

This must be resisted with all the power that public opinion can muster. Everything, yes, everything connected with our 19th-century genius should be preserved.

Traffic wise, I cannot see the need to destroy the G.W.R. office block, when there is shortly to be a gain of several yards depth on the opposite side of the road. If the Brunel offices go, so must W. H. Smith's warehouse – there will be no advantage with one and not the other.

Is the W. H. Smith's building to go? We the citizens of Bristol deserve a full explanation of this scheme.

I and many others who agree with me, will put up with the destruction of unworthy buildings, but anything by Brunel I will not without a fight.

REECE WINSTONE

(322)   10.45am 20 July 1963: Temple Meads Station Plaque erected jointly by Bristol Civic Society and British Railways in 1963 indicates, together with the attempts to have the building listed in the Chronology of Events and John Totterdill's *Masterpiece* in Appendix I, how prudent the Civic Society had been in establishing the importance of the building eight years earlier.

†**(323 & 324)   31 October 1971: Canon's Marsh** By-law had precluded Sunday trading until the popularity of this market site with its ready-made car park and covered area in the former goods depot offended no one.

†(325) Dominican Friary, Quakers Friars The 1230 roof over the rubblestone range, in danger of collapse in 1971, repaired in-situ, completed 1974. A rare, undecorated and early medieval large span roof, predating the subsequent local tradition of raised crucks; a composite form of second tier crucks over arch-braced principals and king-post collar rafter roof. Did this conjunction provide the infirmary with louvre ventilation per bay when ceiled above king posts? Beautifully repaired but the range still unplastered and now threatened with an adjacent shopping mall on city-owned land against the advices of SPAB.

†(326) Castle Vestibule, Castle St Two adjoining vaulted chambers of C13 & C14 seen after conservative repair, before being paved after 1973. Received popularist facelifting externally at the city's behest by others to the chagrin of the repairing architect.

†(327) St Peter's Church, Peter St Blitz'-damaged C15 north aisle fabric under repair from 1971. Excavations in 1975 suggested this is the site of the first city church, hence the suggestion that St Peter's is Bristol's mother church. Another case of a medieval building being left unplastered externally after repair.

(328 & 329) Midday 18 June 1971: Rupert St Failure of the mid-C19 Froom culvert under traffic load. Development of Rupert St mostly takes its cue from the curving river. But not so the severely modern Police & Fire Station of 1928 by Jones and Percy Thomas.

(330) 12.40pm 18 June 1971: Ashton Gate Tollhouse Site clearance preparatory to construction of flats for the elderly by SW Housing Society Ltd, completed 1973. Misgivings were had over the loss of the door. The 'dower house' in Coronation Rd, background, dem. unilaterally *c.*1987 for garage car parking!

†**(331) 1971: Bond St** Paul Mount's 'Spirit of Bristol', having first been declined by another city, has little of the contemporaneity of the Arnolfini pieces [**291**].

(332) 11.10am 10 August 1971: Pen Park Road French Concorde 01 lands at Filton for installation of 5963 mk 602 powerplant. Centre, distance, remains of engine test bed heard over north Bristol for most of the 60's. French and English maiden flights had been in 1969.

1972

†**(333) *c.*1976: Flax Bourton, Post Office Lane houses** Speculative housing by Artist Constructor Ltd, 1972, introduces a new aesthetic in the rural setting and the use of colourwash played a significant part. A group sadly altered by extensions.

Evening Post, Monday, November 6

Place for a box

I was very interested in your story "Who wants a pillar box?".

I would like to suggest that the ideal site for Bristol's oldest post box – the 1865 postbox removed from Ashley Road due to the Parkway roadworks – is alongside the SS *Great Britain*.

Visitors to the ship could post their cards in the box and maybe the Post Office could collect the cards in a special mailbag for them to be franked with an SS *Great Britain* stamp.

REECE WINSTONE

1973

Evening Post, Tuesday, December 18

Save Brandon Cottage!

Your news item that the Savages' former home is looking neglected prompts me to ask: why?

This would make a first class home, temporarily, for students, permanently, when modernised to sell for £20,000–£40,000 at today's prices.

Will it be demolished and some faceless, repulsive, 1984 type of office block take its place?

Is there no one within the City Council who is responsible to save this heritage of Bristol? Why do we not employ a paid officer (like the Director of the Art Gallery) who has the necessary historic knowledge, taste, and good sense, to put a stop to this sort of thing; who can say to the Planning Department "You must preserve this or that building".

Why should preservation societies be necessary? Why do not our elected representatives have a qualified officer to save the historic buildings of Bristol?

Why must the preservation societies continually plead to the Central Government for the protection of our local heritage?

What right has the City Council of 1973 to demolish precious examples of architecture of 1773? What will our descendants of 2073, 2173, etc., think of our Council destroying the heritage of beautiful Bristol?

It is not only the 18th century Unitarian Chapel in Lewins Mead and Christmas Steps that are in danger: Here is a first class example of "Strawberry Hill Gothick", Brandon Cottage, going before our very eyes.

Wake up, Bristol District Council, and appoint an Amenity Officer forthwith.

REECE WINSTONE

*(334)   December 1973: Off Hallen Road, Severn House   George Repton's c.1820 villa 'combining Gothick, Venetian and Soanian elements with effortless grace' (Gomme). Finally dem. by a developer after many previous attempts to do likewise. Another case of the corporation taking 'the simple view that conservation of private buildings is the responsibility of the owners' (*Architect's Journal* 25 June '75).

(336)   1966: Brandon Cottage [201].

Evening Post, Friday, February 23

A very simple solution for the proper future of the Dock Area? Declare it a Conservation Area!

REECE WINSTONE

arnolfini gallery

(335)   December 1973: Off Hallen Road, Laundry mid 60's: The then owners of Severn House, a convent, had commissioned this utilitarian building on their estate. A building type to which the modern movement was well suited to give expression. Dem. for housing.

†**(337)   May 1973: Anchor Road, W Shed** The Arnolfini's second home where it first drew a wider public. Part of a poster featuring the work of Derek Boshier superimposed to right.

(338)   5.20pm 9 August 1973: HRH Prince Philip with members of SS *Gt Britain* committee admiring the repaired and painted hull.

1974

Evening Post, Thursday, June 20

Restore this Georgian building now

In a recent issue of the "Post" Christmas Steps was referred to twice.

Cllr. Bill Graves lists our unique street as a tourist attraction; and plans are announced for another office block (without today's necessary 50 per cent space for housing) to stretch from Host Street to the Unitarian Chapel – while it seems that historic building is not under this threat, Christmas Street and Steps are obviously affected.

I think the most important aspect of Christmas Steps is for the **immediate** restoration of the early Georgian house at the corner of Host Street and Christmas Steps (opposite the group of three gabled houses).

This splendid bit of our heritage has been wantonly allowed to deteriorate. It shouts to tourists how insensitive the local authority can be for the few little gems that survive; it is ghastly and horrible.

The result of the planners' discussions will be a test case for amenity and tourist attraction.

REECE WINSTONE

Evening Post, Friday, August 30

Gravestones for church museum

The plans announced for the future of Brunswick Square seem to envisage the scrapping of the Unitarian Cemetery.

What will then happen to the burial place of William James Muller, our noted local artist; and even more importantly, the last resting place of Bristol's most famous historian? John Latimer (whose works were recently republished) died only 70 years ago – yet there is no mention of him in your recent news report.

In 1964, 1966 and in 1969 the Poets' Corner of Bristol Cathedral was the scene of remembrance round his memorial tablet, graced by the quill pen, organised by Bristol Archaeological Committee, the cherished idea of the late Frederick C. Jones.

This committee also made a public appeal a few years ago to repair Latimer's grave.

This was successfully carried out, with sufficient funds left over to place a diagram tablet within the portico of Brunswick Chapel, designed by the late John Totterdill, explaining the position of Latimer's grave.

Should the burial place of these two eminent Bristol worthies be disturbed? And will their gravestones eventually find their way to St Nicholas Church Museum?

REECE WINSTONE

*(339, 340, 341, 342)   September 1974: Kingsdown, St Paul's and poster in Upper Maudlin Street** The Bristol Joint Housing Action Campaign drew attention to the number of empty houses by means of fly posting, daubing slogans and holding public meetings. A self-help housing association resulted but this, like the other housing associations, never grasped the nettle of conservation in refurbishing run-down housing or in the re-use of historic buildings.

*(343)   June 1974: 33/49 Victoria St Bristol Joint Housing Action Campaign occupied a newly completed office development by Mithras Properties Ltd, entering with keys at 10.30pm on 31 May and staying for three weeks. The Housing Action Campaign was able to occupy offices here and properties elsewhere and successfully avoided prosecution through the abilities of the law students on its committee. Although legislation to register empty council property was only brought in in the 80's the Housing Action Campaign was successful in the 70's in moving the City Council to impose a moratorium on further office development which held for the remaining two years of the Labour council. The following year 1000 houses were built, a ten-fold increase. It showed that direct action worked.

*(344) 1974: The Hartcliffe Project; W D & H O Wills HQ in the making. Levels 1 and 2 carry five storeys of offices overlooking an area to be made an artificial lake. Distant, Western Division manufactory; the enormous roof trusses designed by British consultants to be cable-stayed. Unfortunately considered too adventurous by their American counterparts and joint designers, with a jumbled result.

*(345) 1976: The Hartcliffe Project; Head Office from the west. Management dining rooms over research laboratories overlook a dammed pigeon house stream. Five storeys of offices constructed in CorTen weathering steel, as was Western Division manufactory, left, and the road bridge on Hengrove Way. A *tour de force* of corporate confidence, the American experience applied to green field sites and now threatened with asset stripping.

*(346) 1974: The Hartcliffe Project; Western Division Primary where tobacco leaf was processed prior to rolling.

*(347) December 1974: Lower Cheltenham Place, Montpelier The garden side of this listed row of late Georgian artisan houses. Blighted by proposals for a new school before Avon County took over responsibility for schools under reorganisation on 1 January 1974. Saved from demolition at public inquiry by the CPAB and subsequently left to rot. Altered when saved at the last moment in 1988 with urban grant.

*(348) September 1974: Barton Hill, 42 Queen Anne Rd Late C19 works accessed through a hauling-way in a late C19 terrace of houses; shopfront at No. 42.

*(349) September 1974: Chapel St, Easton Chapel St Flats; early C20 local authority 'walk-ups' or flats with balcony access, eight flats per side of the court.

1975

Evening Post, Tuesday, August 26

Use unique church for housing

How dare Bristol Corporation demolish the Victorian Church of St Gabriel's – only because they have allowed it to be broken into.

Let them make it safe (as they should have done years ago) and put it to a good community use – housing, a Corporation committee meeting room, a pub even.

Can't they recognise a unique polychromatic brick design by J. C. Neale of 1870?

Don't they realise this building is an example of "Bristol Byzantine" and has more character than a hundred of the ugly office towers they permit to scar the centre of our once lovely city.

Thank goodness the Department of the Environment has listed the church!

REECE WINSTONE

Evening Post, Thursday, September 4

Historian hits out on church listing

Bristol historian Mr Reece Winstone today urged more listing of buildings by the Government following the "hasty" demolition of St Gabriel's Church, Easton.

It was demolished last week-end, weeks after it had been listed by the Environment Department, because the City Council considered it dangerous.

Mr Winstone writes in a letter to the Evening Post:

"The more one studies the Corporation's attitude, the more one is grateful that listing of important buildings is being carried out by the Department of the Environment.

"Perhaps our planners don't seem to realise that there must be a very good reason for the Department's action."

Mr Winstone also questions whether Church authorities made determined efforts to find an alternative use for the church.

Diocesan Secretary Cmdr. Herbert Jemphrey said today: "Every effort was made to find another use for the building but we couldn't find anyone willing to take it over.

"By Church rules we have to leave a church standing for a year in case anything does develop. The Corporation served a Dangerous Structure Order and decided to demolish it."

He said the church had been subject to "ghastly vandalism".

Mrs Hazel Kelshaw, wife of the Rev. Terence Kelshaw, who had care of the church, said today: "We did not want to see it pulled down but it became too dangerous."

City public relations officer Mr Tony Trott today said that the building was listed 23 days after the city issued a demolition order.

"The local authority considered it a public danger and took immediate action."

*(350)   July 1975: Castlemead House, Penn St from Kingsdown Parade: A lightning strike over the Town & Commercial Hotels Ltd incomplete office development.

*(351)   November 1975: The Portway during closure for resurfacing the loose Lower Dolomite in the overthrust. Quietude descended on St Vincent's Pde for the duration and the roadway was used for recreation.

*(352) March 1975: Narrow Lewin's Mead Left, the remains of St Bartholomew's Hospital, founded 1260, used by Bristol Grammar School from 1532 and QEH until 1847.

*(353) April 1975: Narrow Lewin's Mead The ranges occupied by Burleigh Press printing works, printers of RW's books. Johnny Ball Lane runs up extreme right. The two bays to the left of the door retain their C17 windows inserted in the end of an earlier cross range. The C18 range, heightened in C19, dem. for an office development up to the line of new carriageway in 1984 by Bristol Municipal Charities.

*(354) September 1975: 87 St George's Rd** North side, looking up to the rear of Queen's Pde; the car is parked in St George's Place. A row of three houses dem. c.1977 for a block of flats of unspeakable design.

*(355) March 1975: 15 Christmas Steps** C19 shop front and door to house above all painted black in narrow Christmas Steps when the intention was to draw the eye to the contents of the window rather than the shop front itself. The street has suffered from a surfeit of white replica bows.

*(356) March 1975: Unitarian Chapel, Lewin's Mead** A prison architect's design of 1791 seen here after the development of Greyfriars behind in 1974 dwarfed this substantial chapel. For years under threat, eventually converted to offices with grant aid against advices of the Georgian Group.

*(359) Pembroke St, St Paul's Right, Howard Hatcher Ltd, furniture manufacturers, and cabinet makers left, on the south side. A Georgian house with fine red and black diaper brickwork dem. *c.*1977 in connection with office development (eventually Spectrum by Espley Tyas Properties). Not considered worthy of retention by the City Planning Officer despite the recent designation of outstanding conservation area. Spectrum was just the sort of inappropriate office development that was intended to be precluded by the same designation. The gulf between good practice and decision making was as wide here as anywhere else.

*(360) May 1975: St Paul's St From Dale Street multi-storey car park looking the other way to pl.**358** down into St Paul's St, a good regular Georgian street which was to receive no protection after the conservation area was designated. The west side dem. *c.*1989, including number 3 without prior consent.

*(357) August 1975: Pritchard Street East side late C18 terrace stepping down to Newfoundland Road; once fashionable area entirely given over to commercial use but yet capable of refurbishment. Entirely dem. against all advices and with the approval of the city council and indicative of the vested interests that blight Bristol. Incorrectly rebuilt in replica façades fronting an office block by London & Bristol Dev. Co.

*(358) August 1975: St Paul's St/Newfoundland St Georgian Newfoundland Rd first threatened in the 1966 city centre plan as a corridor to M4. St Paul's St blighted by the determination of property owners to demolish listed buildings knowing that private gain was to be had. Tollgate House, 1975, by Beaverbrook Properties looms overhead.

*(363) **June 1975: Canon's Marsh, Y & Z Sheds;** their roof top cranes removed and a fixed derrick foreground. Note the cast-iron parapets concealing the roofs of these early Mouchel - Hennebique transit sheds. Dem. to aid Lloyds Bank to build offices on city-owned land.

***(361)   May   1975:
Redcliffe   Backs,
Buchanan's warehouse**
Formerly   Proctor
Baker's granary, left,
and mill right, 1883.
Archetypal of the Float,
red in colour, but ill-used
in conversion following
unnecessary demolition
of stack and conveyors.
The   essential   scale
contrast   between
Buchanan's   and
warehouses to left to be
ignored by Standard
Life Assurance Co.'s
development, 1990.

***(362)   April   1975:
Buchanan's warehouse**
from   the   east.   The
loading platforms that
were to be removed and
the interiors kitted out
with replica Georgian
panel doors, all with
benefit of grant aid.

***(364)   May 1975: Gas
Ferry Road** One of the
1880's   *rundbogen*
manufactories for coal
gas alongside a listed,
mid-C19 roadway of
especial   character;
pennant walls, foot-
ways, cast-iron kerbs
and setts (intact till
c.1970).

(365)   5.20pm 28 May 1975:
SS *Gt Britain* HRH Duke of Edinburgh,
Gould Adams & Lord Mayor on a visit to
the ship.

*(366)   1975: St Philip's Marsh
Manufactory east of Victoria Rd shortly
before dem.

***(367)   1975: Victoria Rd, St Philip's
Marsh** Entry to the goods depot
adjacent to the bridge over Victoria Rd.
Red and black brick with bullnose
corners, iron frames, slate roof and glass
canopy bring dignity to a humble
building.

*(368) July 1975: Coronation Road, Gaol bridge, 1935, to replace the chain ferry to Southville. The cranes on Prince's Wharf are those saved by the intervention of CDV Ltd.

*(369) November 1975: Prince's Buildings, Clifton A new garden scheme in progress with the author of the aesthetic pictured.

*(370) Bath Road, Longwell Green Oldland Hall in Kingswood area before it suffered conversion by the developer who substantially demolished Cedar Hall, Frenchay, which the compiler had delisted. A clumsy design of *c*.1820. The setting recently subsumed under suburban houses.

*(372) July 1975: Ashton Court The free pop festival draws a weekend audience. Note the fashion for flared trousers.

†(374) Early morning, 24 November 1975: Chatsworth Rd, Brislington A Bristol VRT double deck chassis leaves Bristol Commercial Vehicles works in background on its delivery drive to the coachbuilders. The works closed 1981 and Eastern Coachworks, Lowestoft, regularly supplied from Bristol in this manner, closed a few years later.

*(371) September 1975: Blackboy Hill An ill-sited speculative office block, where Georgian cottages formerly stood; otherwise a cut above the average and taken by a bank.

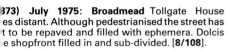

373) July 1975: Broadmead Tollgate House es distant. Although pedestrianised the street has t to be repaved and filled with ephemera. Dolcis e shopfront filled in and sub-divided. **[8/108]**.

†(375) Early morning, 24 November 1975: Chatsworth Rd, Brislington A Bristol LH single deck chassis leaves for the coachworks, the driver with rudimentary protection against the weather.

†(376)   1976: Beaufort Road, Shoreland House
Flats by Artist Constructor bring a new and unmatched standard of design to flats in Clifton but not without falling foul of interference from the planners.

†(377)   1975: Shoreland House test panels. The planners insisted on the fake stone, left, for all work in Clifton and disallowed purpose-made terracotta concrete blocks, centre (surviving in the car park). The RFAC broke the impasse by suggesting terracotta-coloured brick. An example of the planners' ignorance of scale and materials, and their propensity to interfere in matters of design regardless of the ability of the designer.

**(378) March 1975: Johnny
[Bal]l Lane with Colston Yard
[ab]ove** Note the surviving gas
[lan]tern. Decay to right and
[be]hind camera produced the
[so]urce of the best blackberries
[in] central Bristol.

**[Bel]ow *(379) 1975: Lodge
[St]reet** Dem. of the west side
[bli]ghted the east side such
[th]at an office consent was
[en]couraged. The east side
[sav]ed with offer of HBC grant
[for] refurbishment. This did not
[pre]vent principal rooms being
[su]bdivided and Georgian
[win]dos, doors etc. being
[re]moved in 1979.

**[Be]low, right, *(380) April
[19]75: Lower Park Row,
[de]georgianised gable end.** First
[re]alisatiion by the compiler of
[a] Jacobean house surviving at
[10] Lower Park Row. In 1979
[th]e compiler stopped the
[de]molition application and
[fo]und intact Jacobean
[in]teriors! With disinterest
[sh]own by local amenity
[bo]dies, who feared
[je]opardizing the funding of
[Ge]orgian Lodge St, he
[co]nvinced the generous-
[he]arted neighbour to part with
[a] strip of his garden in order to
[pr]ovide light and walkway
[pa]st the frontage, putting a
[re]al obstacle in the way of
[cl]earance. Sadly then poorly
[ref]urbished.

*(381)   May 1975: 16 Victoria Street Oliver's bar formerly a wine merchant's premises by J Michelen Rogers, 1871, and the subject of a long running battle by Victorian Society after Courages vacated the premises and sought demolition consent for part of Bath Street to the rear. This exuberantly decorated building by a Londoner featured the griffin for Bristol (removed without consent and not reinstated) and the lion for Courage (nothing to do with the company) and probably featured two other emblems in the blank circles of the façade. The 1990 appeal decision to permit partial demolition and added storeys to listed buildings adjacent seems likely to have put back conservation in Bristol many years.

*(382)   July 1975: 7 King Square The Palladian coachhouse at the rear, once part of an imposing backdrop extending throughout the terrace and only surviving here. The other surviving Kingsdown coachhouse at 6 Somerset St sadly neglected. Saved at appeal by the compiler in 1989, but requests that the garden should be unparked (as policy requires all Georgian gardens to be) disregarded. Seen before ill-use by former owners and before Montague Court reared its head.

*(383) September 1990: Those familiar with these books may appreciate the inclusion, by now well established, of a family tailpiece, in this instance very up-to-date.

ASHTON COURT RESTRU

ASHTON COURT 'CREATIVE RESTORATION' for The City of Bristol   Illustra